P9-DYB-817

Eritrea

Cavendish Square

New York

Published in 2020 by Cavendish Square Publishing, LLC
243 5th Avenue, Suite 136, New York, NY 10016
Copyright © 2020 by Cavendish Square Publishing, LLC

Third Edition

Website: cavendishsq.com

This publication represents the opinions and views of the author based on his or her personal experience, knowledge, and research. The information in this book serves as a general guide only. The author and publisher have used their best efforts in preparing this book and disclaim liability rising directly or indirectly from the use and application of this book.

All websites were available and accurate when this book was sent to press.

Library of Congress Cataloging-in-Publication Data

Names: NgCheong-Lum, Roseline, 1962- author. | Orr, Tamra, author.
Title: Eritrea / Roseline NgCheong-Lum and Tamra B. Orr.
Description: [Third edition]. | [New York] : [Cavendish Square Publishing], [2020] |
Series: Cultures of the world | Includes bibliographical references and index.
Identifiers: LCCN 2019048231 (print) | LCCN 2019048232 (ebook) |
ISBN 9781502655776 (library binding) | ISBN 9781502655783 (ebook)
Subjects: LCSH: Eritrea--Juvenile literature.
Classification: LCC DT393 .N47 2020 (print) | LCC DT393 (ebook) | DDC 963.5--dc23
LC record available at https://lccn.loc.gov/2019048231
LC ebook record available at https://lccn.loc.gov/2019048232

Editor: Kristen Susienka
Copy Editor: Nathan Heidelberger
Designer: Jessica Nevins

Some of the images in this book illustrate individuals who are models. The depictions do not imply actual situations or events.

CPSIA compliance information: Batch #CS20CSQ: For further information contact Cavendish Square Publishing LLC, New York, New York, at 1-877-980-4450.

Printed in the United States of America

$ 29.66

Find us on

CONTENTS

ERITREA TODAY

IN SEPTEMBER 2018, AN ETHIOPIAN MAN NAMED ASTEBEHA TESFAYE found out that he could finally go home. He had been waiting a very long time. He had traveled to Eritrea in 1998 to visit a friend, when a border war broke out between Ethiopia and Eritrea. Suddenly, Tesfaye could not leave the country. "I was going to take the bus the next day [back to Ethiopia]," he told the *New York Times*, "but I heard that the roads were blocked, and that no one was going to move either to Eritrea or Ethiopia … There wasn't any day that went by that I didn't think of my mother. I never thought this day would come."

Tesfaye was not the only person to rejoice as the two countries' leaders signed a peace agreement. On both sides of the border, people cheered and hugged. Families were reunited. For the first time in 20 years, phone lines were reopened. Brothers called sisters, parents called children, and friends called friends. Commercial flights between Ethiopia and Eritrea were reinstated, and embassies unlocked their doors. It was a monumental moment for the young African state of Eritrea.

THE COUNTRY NOW

Eritrea is located in northeastern Africa, along the Red Sea. It looks like a flower spread out alongside the sea. Its "stem" stretches to the southeast to border Djibouti. It expands into a "flower" at the country's capital city of Asmara, and the "petals" reach out to Ethiopia in the south and Sudan in the west.

The country is a land of extreme contrast. In the central plateau, the soil is rich and fertile, while in the lowlands, desert sand reigns and droughts are common. Asmara's Italian-style modernist architecture, which earned it UNESCO World Heritage status in 2017, exists in the same country as one of the world's only red-hot and bubbling lava lakes. A mountain called Emba Soira soars almost 10,000 feet (3,048 meters) into the clouds, while the Danakil Depression ranks as one of the hottest, driest, and lowest places on the entire planet. With average temperatures of 95 degrees Fahrenheit (35 degrees Celsius), it is a place of little water and lots of camels.

Although Eritrea is one of the youngest independent countries in Africa, the land is actually ancient. The region in which it is found is sometimes referred to as the "cradle of humanity" because of the number and age of fossils found here. In fact, Eritrea has had more than 80,000 archaeological discoveries to date. One notable find is the Buya Woman, named for the area of her discovery. The well-preserved female skull is over 1 million years old and provides important information about the development of early humans.

Almost 6 million people live in Eritrea, a country about the same size as the US state of Mississippi. Some of the ethnic groups within Eritrea can trace their origins back to before 2000 BCE. Most people live in the rural areas of the country, working as farmers and shepherds. There is no national or official language, but instead the people speak more than 10 languages. From English to the main dialect of Tigrinya, each one is considered equal, as stated in the country's constitution.

FREEDOM FIGHTERS

For decades, Eritreans have had to fight for their freedom. At first, it was oppression by Italian colonialists, whose influence is scattered throughout many of the buildings in cities like Asmara. Then, Britain took control for another decade. After that, the people of Eritrea had to battle against neighboring Ethiopia, a fight that made progress toward resolution in 2018. It is the only country in the world where elections keep being scheduled and then canceled. No elections have actually been held in Eritrea since the country gained its independence in 1993. The same president has ruled since that year.

Eritrea faces many different challenges, from rising sea levels and recurring droughts caused by climate change to maintaining international respect. In 2019, the African nation was voted "the most censored country in the world." Along with North Korea and Turkmenistan, Eritrea does not allow independent reporters to discuss what is happening throughout the nation. It also refuses to allow foreign journalists into the country. Those who do make it in are typically imprisoned. Instead, all journalists in Eritrea must work for the state and will traditionally be told what to report—or what not to report. The people's view of the world is often skewed by the inability to hear other ideas and information. Less than 2 percent of Eritreans are able to go online, and the country has the lowest rate of cell phone ownership in the world.

Religious freedom is also a challenge in Eritrea. The country refuses to recognize any religious group other than Sunni Islam, Eritrean Orthodox Christian, Roman Catholic, and Protestant. Homes where other religions are practiced are often raided by security officers. Offenders who refuse to immediately convert are jailed indefinitely. In 2019, Eritrean authorities took control of seven schools run by religious organizations outside of those that were sanctioned, or approved. The schools were given to the approved religious groups to run instead.

Eritreans have fought for decades for their independence and want to hang on to it. Like others around the world, they are willing to work hard to create a secure future for themselves and their families. They have some serious obstacles to overcome in the process. Climate change is going to transform their land, and continued government control may make them consider joining the many refugees who leave for brighter prospects.

Eritrea today is evolving. It may have some significant obstacles to overcome, but it is also making strides. Just ask Astebeha Tesfaye, who is happy to be home.

GEOGRAPHY

Eritrea is a place filled with diverse geography,
such as the mountains near Massawa, seen here.

1

ON THE NORTHEASTERN COAST OF Africa, at the top edge of the Horn of Africa, is Eritrea. The shape of the country is often compared to a funnel or a flower. At 45,406 square miles (117,600 square kilometers), it is about the same size as Mississippi and one of the smaller countries on the continent. Eritrea borders three other nations. Sudan is to the northwest, Djibouti to the southeast, and Ethiopia to the south. Its northeastern border runs along the Red Sea for more than 715 miles (1,151 km). In fact, the country gets its name from the Latin name for the Red Sea, *mare erythraeum*. For years, Eritrea's location was the envy of other nearby landlocked nations. Its long coastline made it the perfect stop for ships coming and going on the international trade route.

In his book *Inside Africa* (1955), John Gunther called Eritrea "a thorny, forlorn splinter of desert-cum-mountain along the Red Sea."

This map shows Eritrea's land borders with Sudan, Ethiopia, and Djibouti, and its 715-mile (1,151 km) coastline along the Red Sea.

In addition to its mainland, Eritrea also has many small islands dotting the Red Sea. Over 100 islands make up the Dahlak Archipelago. Of those islands, only four are inhabited by people. However, sea birds from all over the world take shelter on many of the smaller islands, and tourists enjoy diving and boating around the archipelago.

INTO THE ZONES

Eritrea can be divided into three main zones: the fertile, farmed central plateau (also known as the central highlands); the semiarid western lowlands; and the desert-like coastal plain. Each region has its own unique terrain, climate, and soil.

The central plateau is a narrow strip of land that runs through the middle of the country. It is an extension of the Ethiopian Plateau in the south. The plateau rises to 6,500 feet (1,980 m) above sea level. At its northern end, it narrows into a system of eroded hills. Rivers flow through the central highlands, carving deep gorges and small plateaus called *ambas* (AHM-bahs).

The central plateau's higher elevation means that the temperatures are not so blisteringly hot, and more rain falls there than in other parts of Eritrea. Those factors combine to create fertile soil. In turn, this rich soil attracts farmers and crops. Although the central highlands make up only a quarter of the country's total land area, approximately half of all Eritreans live here. This area includes Central region and is where the cities Asmara and Keren are located.

The broken and undulating western plain slopes gradually toward the border with Sudan. It lies at an average elevation of 1,500 feet (457 m). Unlike the central plateau, this region has sandy soil that cannot hold on to water. The main types of growth here include scattered trees, shrubs, and grasses.

Eritrea's coastal plain stretches along the Red Sea between the borders with Djibouti and Sudan. This zone takes up one-third of Eritrea's total land area and encompasses the Northern Red Sea and Southern Red Sea Zones. The coastal plain falls sharply from the central plateau and is narrower in the north—10 to 50 miles (16 to 80 km) wide—than in the south, where it widens to include the Danakil (sometimes spelled Denakil) Plain. This barren region is part of the Danakil Depression, which Eritrea shares with Ethiopia. The coastal plain is part of the East African Rift System, a deep valley running from Tanzania in the south to the Red Sea, created around 25 million years ago by the collision of tectonic plates. The coastal plain suffers from poor soil quality and supports little vegetation. The main towns in this zone are the port cities of Massawa and Assab.

Lush green areas are relatively rare in arid, hot Eritrea.

AN ARCHIPELAGO

Eritrea's Red Sea area is made up of the Dahlak Archipelago and a scattering of other islands and islets. Dahlak Kebir, the largest island in the Dahlak Archipelago, has an area of only 248 square miles (643 sq km). About 60 percent of the 2,500 people living on these islands make a living fishing and herding cattle.

Because the Dahlak Archipelago is so remote and has so few people, it is teeming with marine life, including dolphins, sharks, dugongs, turtles, hermit crabs, and jellyfish. Mangroves, shoals, coral reefs, and pumice stone formed from underwater volcanoes all contribute to its designation as a national park. The Red Sea's warm water also makes this area a colorful haven for more than 1,000 species of fish and coral, luring in tourists and scuba divers from all over the world.

FROM HIGH TO LOW

Eritrean terrain is mountainous with tremendous topographical variation. The highest point in the country is Emba Soira, one of several mountains in the highlands. It rises to a height of 9,902 feet (3,018 m). The lowest point, 246 feet (75 m) below sea level, is inside the Kobar Sink in the Danakil Depression.

Eritrea is so dry that its rivers come and go with the seasons. The only river that flows year round is the Tekeze River, also called the Setit. It flows along the Ethiopian border and into Sudan, where it joins the Atbara River and ultimately the Nile. During the rainy season, the Barka and Anseba Rivers flow north to the eastern coast of Sudan but stop short of reaching the Red Sea. The Gash crosses the western lowlands, and its upper course, known as the Mereb, flows along the Ethiopian border on the plateau.

THE WEATHER REPORT

The climate in Eritrea depends largely on the altitude. The central plateau experiences a moderate climate with highs of 86°F (30°C) in May and near-freezing lows in December through February. In the western lowlands' hottest months—traditionally April, May, and June—it can reach 106°F (41°C). During the coolest month, December, temperatures average 55°F (13°C). On the coastal plain, winter temperatures range between 70°F (21°C) and 95°F (35°C), while the summer—from June to September—sees temperatures rising as high as 122°F (50°C). The Danakil Depression is the hottest place in the country.

The Danakil Depression is so dry that it almost looks like an alien landscape.

The amount of rain varies across the nation too. The "short rains" fall in March and April, while the main rains last from late June to early September. The central plateau experiences the most rain, with an annual average of 16 to 20 inches (40.6 to 50.8 centimeters). The western lowlands receive less than 16 inches (40.6 cm) a year, while the coastal plain is far drier.

The inner parts of the Danakil Plain are virtually rainless. Sprawling across the Eritrean-Ethiopian border near Djibouti, this region is one of the most inhospitable places on Earth. This dramatic landscape of deserts, rocks, salt formations, and black volcano cones is one of the lowest places on Earth not covered by water. Across the border in Ethiopia, it reaches a maximum depth of 410 feet (125 m) below sea level. The plain boasts the world's hottest place as well. The Ethiopian town of Dallol experiences an annual mean temperature of 94°F (34°C). The blistering sun and strong winds make survival here impossible for most plants and animals.

The little Eritrean village of Badda serves as a gateway to the Danakil Depression. The fertile land here supports the cultivation of crops. Sunday markets attract camel caravans from across the moonlike Danakil Plain, although sandstorms, which strike daily between 1:00 p.m. and 4:00 p.m., reduce visibility to less than 33 feet (10 m). The village's main attraction, however, is the turquoise Lake Badda. It sits in an ancient volcano crater around 1,313 feet (400 m) wide and 328 feet (100 m) deep.

A LOOK AT THE WILDLIFE

Decades of armed conflict and recurrent drought have taken a heavy toll on Eritrea's natural world. The massive destruction of tropical forests, accompanied by illegal hunting, resulted in the near extinction of many plant and animal species. Upon independence, the government initiated strict measures to restore the country's ecological environment. Captive breeding, land reservation, reforestation, and public awareness campaigns have been successful, and the country's formerly abundant flora and fauna are on the road to recovery.

Trees and other plants growing in Eritrea include baobab, pine, eucalyptus, olive, aloe, and sisal. Some, like the tamarind tree, are on the endangered list.

Shrubs and grasses associated with the savanna add shades of green to the western lowlands. Tropical flowering plants, especially acacia, bougainvillea, and jacaranda, beautify all the major towns. The national flower is the brightly colored gerbera daisy. Discovered in 1884 in South Africa, this flower grows in multiple colors and brightens the landscapes after a rainstorm.

Efforts to preserve the country's animal diversity have resulted in the return of elephants, leopards, gazelles, antelopes, wild hogs and donkeys, hyenas, and ostriches. Smaller animals that have made a comeback include rabbits, rodents, and monkeys. There are also the fish and birds of the Red Sea islands. More than 100 bird species feed on sardines and anchovies migrating through the Red Sea. Sheep, goats, cattle, and domesticated camels are raised by farmers and shepherds. The camel has been adopted as the national emblem for its significant role in transporting supplies during the war for independence.

One of the biggest pests found in Eritrea are locusts. These migratory insects compete with humans for food as they attack a wide range of crops and trees. They are able to eat amounts of food equal to their own body weight every

As small as locusts are, they can do astounding damage in a short period of time, especially in a land where food resources are already limited.

day. This means a swarm of 40 million locusts can eat the same amount of food in 24 hours as 35,000 people could! Locusts can wipe out entire crops, taking everything that farmers have been able to grow. They are also able to travel from 60 to 250 miles (96 to 402 km) a day, so they can cover huge areas of land.

In 2019, Saudi Arabia and nearby lands, including Eritrea, were hit by a particularly large swarm of desert locusts. Thanks to heavier rains than usual, two generations were able to breed, resulting in billions of insects. Attacks were so thick that they looked like huge storm clouds able to cover several hundred square miles.

Eritrea has a diverse landscape, where the Danakil Depression exists along with a big city like Asmara, shown here.

LITTLE ROME

Perched 1.5 miles (2.4 km) high on the central plateau is Asmara, Eritrea's capital city and a UNESCO World Heritage city. Often referred to as "Little Rome," Asmara became the capital of Eritrea in 1897 when the Italian colonial authorities decided to shift their administrative center here, away from the sweltering heat of the coastal town of Massawa. With a population of about 564,000 today, Asmara is the largest city in the country.

The name Asmara comes from *arbate asmara*, which means "they united the four." According to legend, when fighting broke out among four small villages in the region, the village women collaborated to unite their people. Another legend says that the Queen of Sheba bore King Solomon a son in this area.

Unlike most capital cities on the African continent, Asmara is safe enough for residents and tourists to roam the streets both day and night. The city features a large central market that sells vegetables, spices, clothing, baskets, and pottery, among other items. The heart of the city is Liberation Avenue, where cafés and bars abound. In the evenings, residents walk along the avenue, sip coffee in the cafés, and shop in the stores.

Much of the city was built in the 1920s and 1930s, during Italy's rule. There are some tall buildings in the city center, but most houses, such as the old Italian villas, are one or two stories high. Art deco and modernist styles still decorate the city, including the futurist Fiat Tagliero Building, a former gas station. One of the oldest and most beautiful buildings in Asmara is the former Governor's Palace, built in 1897. Until 1997, it was home to the National Museum. The museum has since moved, but the palace remains a main tourist attraction. Among Asmara's many important buildings and places are the High Court, the City Hall, the National Bank, the Catholic Church of Our Lady of the Rosary, the Khulafa el-Rashidin Mosque, and the Enda Mariam Orthodox Church.

Italians left their mark in ways beyond architecture. Pizza and pasta are still served throughout the city. Italy also introduced the area to bicycle racing, and it has become a great passion in Asmara.

AROUND THE COUNTRY

Keren is the second-largest city, after Asmara. Nestled amid mountains, Keren, which means "highland," sits 4,567 feet (1,392 m) up on a plateau and is home to 74,800 people. It has a large Muslim population and many mosques. The lively market here attracts traders from the region, who haggle over camels, donkeys, and sheep. Keren was severely damaged in the country's struggle for independence.

About 62 miles (100 km) east of Asmara, Massawa is the country's main port and its third-largest city, with 23,100 people. It was once called the "Pearl of the Red Sea," but its glory is fading. It is the largest natural deepwater port on the Red Sea coast. Causeways link the mainland part of Massawa to two islands, Batse (also known as Massawa Island) and Taulud. The port itself is on the island of Batse. Because of Massawa's strategic coastal location, it has always been an important trading center. It, too, suffered heavy shelling by the Ethiopians during the war for independence, but it is now back in operation. Thanks to its beautiful beaches, Massawa is a popular weekend destination for many families.

Before the border conflict with Ethiopia began in 1998, Assab used to be landlocked Ethiopia's gateway to the Red Sea. Ethiopian traders brought prosperity to the town and turned it into Eritrea's largest port. During the war with Ethiopia, the government denied its use to Ethiopia, and although it is rebuilding today, the town had been in decline for years.

Nakfa is special in every Eritrean's heart, for it was the first town to be recaptured by liberation fighters from the Ethiopian forces in the 1970s. The national currency was named after Nakfa in 1997 to commemorate the significance of the town in the country's history.

Other cities throughout Eritrea include Mendefera and Barentu. Mendefera has a population of approximately 17,700 and is full of rolling hills. The city was built during the Italian occupation. Where it was once a thick jungle, it is now a busy market town. Barentu, home to about 15,900, is in the western lowlands. It is hot, and many nomadic tribes live in this one-street town. One of the smallest cities in the nation is Quandeba. Located about 12 miles (20 km) from Asmara, this small place is home to only about 1,000 people.

INTERNET LINKS

https://www.britannica.com/place/Eritrea
Interesting facts and details about Eritrea are located at this website.

https://www.cia.gov/library/publications/the-world-factbook/geos/er.html
The *CIA World Factbook* provides key information about Eritrea, from its geography to its economy.

https://www.worldatlas.com/webimage/countrys/africa/eritrea/erland.htm
Details about Eritrea's geography can be found here.

https://www.youtube.com/watch?v=szOlmgTmfvQ
Seven unique facts about Eritrea are offered on this YouTube video.

HISTORY

Amazing archaeological findings have
been located in all parts of Eritrea.

2

ALMOST 2 MILLION YEARS AGO, *HOMO erectus*, or "upright man," developed in eastern Africa. With a small brain and large teeth, this species figured out how to control fire. *Homo erectus* fossils have been found throughout Africa, as well as in western and central Asia, China, and Indonesia. They may have also inhabited Europe. In Eritrea's inhospitable Danakil Depression, a slab of stone was buried under the sand until a team of researchers found it in 2016. They were astounded to spot a set of *Homo erectus* footprints impressed into the rock.

These ancient footprints are only one example of the countless archaeological discoveries made in Eritrea. From rock paintings to tools, so much has been found throughout the area that it is easy to see why Eritrea is sometimes referred to as part of the cradle of the human species.

FIRST PEOPLE

The first people to settle in the area came from the region of the Nile. These Nilotes occupied the northern parts of Eritrea. Later, migrants from

Archaeologist Alfredo Coppa states, "Footprints will reveal a lot about the evolution of man, because they provide vital information about our ancestors' gait and locomotion."

the ancient North African kingdom of Cush (also spelled Kush) inhabited the Eritrean highlands. By 1000 BCE or earlier, Semites crossed the Red Sea from the South Arabian kingdom of Sheba and invaded the lands of the Cushitic settlers. The Semitic occupants introduced the ancient Geez script, the root of some of the languages used in Eritrea today. They also brought camels and sheep and developed irrigation systems and hillslope terraces, thus laying Eritrea's agricultural foundations and setting the stage for the reign of the Aksumites, the first of many "outsiders" to rule Eritrea for the next three millennia before its independence.

A POWERFUL KINGDOM

Spanning from the first century to the eighth century CE, the Kingdom of Aksum rose to prominence in the fourth and fifth centuries. It stretched from Nubia (now Sudan) into Somalia, and across the Red Sea into southern Arabia (now Yemen). Its capital city was in Ethiopia, but it had important towns in Eritrea as well. Aksum controlled the land and sea routes from Africa to Europe and Asia, and it monopolized trade in the region. Its principal port, Adulis (now Zula), was a trading center for gold, gems, incense, and other goods.

The Aksumites are known for several achievements during their reign in Eritrea. One king, Ezana, is believed to have introduced Christianity to the region. Victory over the Jewish king of Yemen, who persecuted Christians, and the arrival of Syrian missionaries, who contributed significantly to local religious practices, earned Aksum great prestige and consolidated its position as a powerful defender of Christianity. However, Adulis was destroyed in 710 CE by Muslims. For the next few centuries, Eritrea was fought over by both Ethiopian dynasties and Muslim sultanates. Traces of Aksum's great civilization can still be seen today, especially in UNESCO's Ethiopian World Heritage site named after them.

TUG OF WAR

The Ottoman Turks entered Eritrean history in the 16th century, amid a backdrop of feuding kingdoms in the region. They occupied the Eritrean coast in

1517 and took control of Massawa. However, the Portuguese and Abyssinians combined forces to take Massawa from them in 1543. For the next 20 years, control of Massawa alternated between the Turks and these opposing forces. The Turkish leader then ruled most of Eritrea for 15 years alongside the Abyssinian emperor, until the latter beheaded the former. What followed was another tug-of-war between the Turks and the Abyssinians. Finally, in 1589, the Turks agreed to a peace deal with the Abyssinians and remained as a power in Eritrea for another three centuries.

Ottoman buildings are crumbling but still standing in the city of Massawa.

In the middle of the 19th century, the Egyptians became a threat to the region. They invaded Sudan in 1820 and reached Ethiopia in 1840. In 1846, they stepped onto Eritrean shores by signing a lease for Massawa. By 1853, they had conquered the western lowlands and the area around Keren, and by 1875, they had occupied more territory on the coast. However, Egyptian power in the region faded as Egypt came under the British protectorate in the 1880s.

THE EUROPEAN CHAPTER

The Italians came to Africa after the French and the British had secured their presence in the region. They established their administration in Assab in 1882 and ousted the Egyptians from Massawa three years later. A few years after that, they raised their flag in Keren and Asmara. By 1889, the Italians held most of Eritrean land, and the next year, they proclaimed the territory an Italian colony and officially named it Eritrea. Desiring Ethiopia, the Italians clashed with the Abyssinians at Adwa in 1896. The latter became the first African power to defeat a European army. The two sides later signed a treaty recognizing Italian rule over Eritrea. In 1898, Signor Martini became Eritrea's first civilian governor, and by 1910 the colony's provincial structure was in place.

From 1881 to 1914, much of Europe participated in "The Scramble for Africa," a systematic invasion and occupation of African territories. This was during a time period when European countries wanted to expand, and the best way to do so was by seeking opportunities abroad. Africa was a large continent with plenty of land. Countries such as Italy, the United Kingdom, Germany, Belgium, and Spain rushed there, setting up colonies and proclaiming political dominance. All African nations objecting to this invasion could do little to prevent it. Thanks to having advanced weapons, such as machine guns, the Europeans usually overcame any resistance.

In 1940, Great Britain hosted a Sunday parade in Eritrea.

The Italians built railroads, ports, plantations, and factories and introduced modern ways of living in their colony. Eritrea soon overtook Ethiopia in material progress. By 1929, Massawa was the biggest port on the east coast of Africa. By 1937, Eritrea was the center of a regional transportation network employing around 100,000 people.

MOVING TOWARD FEDERATION

In 1935, the Italians launched a planned attack on Ethiopia from their Eritrean base. Six years later, during World War II, the British forced them back into Eritrea. The Italians lost several towns in a matter of months. The Italian surrender of Asmara on April 1, 1941, sealed their defeat in Eritrea, which now faced a new master.

The British were unprepared to run a new administration, and so they made few (though substantial) changes to the current one. They retained the Italian officials, but trained Eritreans in civil service and education. A new curriculum offered classes in agriculture, woodworking, clay-modeling, carpet-making, shoemaking, reading, writing, and hygiene for boys. Girls were offered courses in hygiene, reading, writing, weaving, sewing, basketwork, and domestic science.

The British continued to invest only while Eritrea remained useful to their North African strategy. Toward the end of World War II, in 1944, they began removing infrastructure, equipment, and remaining supplies. Eritrea's economy collapsed in 1946, plunging the country into a state of social unrest.

MISINFORMATION AND PROTEST

During the crisis, Ethiopia intended to annex Eritrea, while the British proposed to partition the country between Sudan and Ethiopia. Eritrea's future became the subject of international debate at the United Nations (UN). To find out what the Eritreans themselves wanted for their future, the UN sent a fact-finding mission to Eritrea. However, the Commission of Enquiry, which was fed misinformation by the British, reported on June 28, 1949, that the Christian majority in Eritrea was in favor of union with Ethiopia.

Emperor Haile Selassie of Ethiopia ruled from 1930 to 1974 and was often equated to God by his followers.

On December 2, 1950, the UN passed a resolution to join Eritrea with Ethiopia. Eritrea would be an autonomous unit governing itself under the sovereignty of Ethiopia. The federal plan took effect on September 11, 1952.

It was not long before the Ethiopian emperor, Haile Selassie, began violating the act of federation. He increasingly interfered in the federal government's administration, banning Eritrean political parties and trade unions and replacing the major languages of Tigrinya and Arabic with Amharic, Ethiopia's official language. Within a decade, the Selassie regime systematically annexed Eritrea, overwhelming its federal government and imposing the regime's own law in the federation.

Eritrea lost its federal status for good in November 1962, becoming Ethiopia's 14th province. The angry Eritreans had no way to fight back. Protesters suffered at the hands of the police and were jailed or forced into exile. Getting outside help was impossible, as their head of state was Selassie's own son-in-law. The only solution seemed to be armed struggle, a reality Eritrea would face for the next 30 years.

FORMING MOVEMENTS

The Ethiopian regime in Eritrea razed villages, kidnapped and killed innocent people, jailed or exiled political leaders, drained economic resources, and displaced hundreds of thousands of people, many of whom sought refuge in neighboring Sudan. Political parties were banned. Newspapers were censored. Protests turned into brawls.

In 1960, exiled Eritreans in Cairo, Egypt, formed the Eritrean Liberation Front (ELF) to raise arms against the Ethiopians. The ELF received enthusiastic support from disgruntled Eritrean workers and students, and soon the revolution spread to the central highlands in Eritrea. However, internal disagreements caused some members to withdraw and form another movement, which would later be named the Eritrean People's Liberation Front (EPLF).

Although the two liberation fronts continued to fight one another—even when Selassie was overthrown in Ethiopia in 1974 and replaced by a new military dictator—they joined forces as a team and succeeded in freeing most of the Eritrean towns from Ethiopia's grip. In fact, they might have won full

Young troops train at an Eritrean People's Liberation Front camp in 1978.

control over Eritrea, if not for the delivery of new armaments to Ethiopia in 1977 by the Soviet Union. Within a year, the Ethiopian regime had regained most of Eritrea, and the ELF and the EPLF were forced to retreat and start again. Only the EPLF survived, fed by a steady flow of Eritreans eager to fight for their freedom. The EPLF fought the bloody war against Ethiopia for another decade, reclaiming Eritrea town by town. When the Soviet Union withdrew its military aid to Ethiopia in the late 1980s, Ethiopia fell. In May 1991, the EPLF assumed complete control over Eritrea.

FINALLY, FREEDOM

At 10:00 a.m. on May 24, 1991, the people of Asmara suddenly realized that EPLF fighters had liberated the city. They threw open their doors and ran into the streets to dance—some still in their pajamas. For the first time in more than 100 years, they were free.

The EPLF established a provisional government and held a national referendum in April 1993 to conclude the country's struggle for freedom. Almost everyone who voted chose independence, and on May 24, 1993, Eritrea was formally declared independent. Relations with Ethiopia started out smoothly, owing to the close friendship between the new Eritrean and Ethiopian leaders. As a gesture of goodwill, Eritrea guaranteed Ethiopian access to the Red Sea through the port of Assab. This privilege was later withdrawn when hostilities erupted over border disputes.

BACK TO BATTLING

In 1997, relations between the two neighbors soured when Ethiopia drew up a new map that placed parts of southwest Eritrea in Ethiopian territory. Fighting broke out in 1998 as each side tried to capture the disputed land. A truce brokered by US and Italian mediators halted the fighting at the end of 1998, but a few months later, the two sides clashed again. In May 2000, Ethiopia occupied large parts of Eritrea, and in June that year, both sides agreed to a cease-fire. A peace agreement was signed under the auspices of the UN in

THE PERMANENT COURT OF ARBITRATION

When two states or countries are battling each other, it is often the Permanent Court of Arbitration (PCA) that makes the big decisions. Established in 1899, the PCA became the first permanent intergovernmental organization for the resolution of international disputes. It is made up of three parts. The Administrative Council oversees policies and budgets. The Members of the Court are independent potential arbitrators or judges. They serve for six years and are selected not only for their competency in international law but also for their "highest moral reputation." There is a separate branch for environmental disputes, as well as one for space-related disputes. The International Bureau is made up of legal and administrative experts from many different countries. It is in charge of communications and the handling and custody of documents.

December. During the two-year war, more than 1 million people were displaced, and an estimated 80,000 lost their lives.

Under the terms of the peace agreement, a 4,200-strong multinational peacekeeping force was deployed in the disputed area to monitor a 15.5-mile- (25 km) wide Temporary Security Zone along the border. In 2002, the Permanent Court of Arbitration in The Hague published its decision on the border dispute, but Ethiopia declined to implement the decision without further negotiations, which the Eritreans rejected. Subsequently, in 2007, the Eritrea-Ethiopia Boundary Commission remotely demarcated the border by coordinates, leaving Ethiopia still occupying several tracts of disputed territory. Eritrea accepted the "virtual demarcation," but Ethiopia rejected it.

PEACE AT LAST

The standoff with Ethiopia over territory continued for years, with occasional outbreaks of violence. For example, more than 200 soldiers were killed in a clash along the border in June 2016. Finally, in July 2018, the two states agreed to end their war. Ethiopian prime minister Abiy Ahmed and Eritrean president Isaias Afwerki signed a peace deal, reopening the border between the two countries. "The state of war between Ethiopia and Eritrea has come to an end," they stated in a joint declaration. "A new era of peace and friendship has been opened." One woman stated to the British Broadcasting Corporation (BBC), "It's a wonderful day. I came here to meet my relatives who I haven't seen for 20 years. We are so happy." Another woman said, "I have met my mother and my siblings after 24 years. I am so happy. I can't express my joy." For his efforts in bringing the border conflict to an end, Prime Minister Abiy Ahmed won the Nobel Peace Prize in 2019.

The border war between Ethiopia and Eritrea that began in 1998 was sometimes described as "two bald men fighting over a comb."

INTERNET LINKS

https://www.bbc.com/news/world-africa-45475876
Read about how people reacted to the border between Ethiopia and Eritrea opening at BBC News.

https://pca-cpa.org/en/home
Learn more about the Permanent Court of Arbitration and what they do at their official website.

https://timelines.ws/countries/ERITREA.HTML
Explore more of Eritrea's history here. The website has a complete, up-to-date, and detailed timeline for the country.

https://www.youtube.com/watch?v=FKRaM_2bcCE
This video explores the long conflict between Ethiopia and Eritrea.

GOVERNMENT

Isaias Afwerki has been president of Eritrea since 1993 and has often been a controversial leader.

3

ON MAY 23, 1993, THE PEOPLE OF Asmara gathered on the city's streets and inside bars to sing, dance, and hug each other in celebration. After three decades of fighting for their independence, they were on their way to seceding from Ethiopia. More than 1.1 million people had participated in a referendum over three days in April, and 99.8 percent had voted in favor of independence. On May 24, then the youngest state in Africa, Hagere Ertra (State of Eritrea), was proclaimed independent. One diplomat in Eritrea stated, "Eritrea will be the most stable country in East Africa until the end of the century, if not longer." To emphasize the change in their nation's status, the government was reorganized into the People's Front for Democracy and Justice (PFDJ).

Isaias Afwerki became president on June 8, 1993, and has held on to the title since then. He also serves as commander in chief of the army and chairman of the country's only political party.

THE THREE BRANCHES

Eritrea's government is made up of three branches: executive, legislative, and judicial. President Isaias Afwerki, the country's first and only president, is part of the executive branch. He and his cabinet of 18 ministers, referred to as the State Council, are in charge of implementing government policies, laws, and regulations. The council includes ministers for the areas of finance, defense, education, tourism, and agriculture. According to the country's constitution, the president is supposed to be elected every five years by the members of the country's legislature. However, no such election has occurred since 1993.

The legislative branch is known as the National Assembly. The constitution says it is to be made up of 75 representatives from the PFDJ, plus 75 members who are elected by a majority vote. However, no elections have been held. The 75 representatives meant to be chosen by voters were instead appointed in 1997. They were drawn from a different assembly that had been formed that year to approve Eritrea's constitution. Women hold 22 percent of the seats in the National Assembly, and 15 seats are reserved to represent the interests of Eritreans who are living abroad.

The judicial branch consists of courts at national, regional, district, and village levels. The highest court of appeal is called the High Court, and the president appoints its judges. There are also 683 community courts spread throughout Eritrea. Cases are heard by more than 2,000 judges. Special sharia courts, which follow Islamic law, cater to the Muslim population.

The judicial branch is nominally independent of the legislative and executive arms of the government. The Ministry of Justice oversees a three-tier legal structure—the High Court, regional courts and subregional courts, and community courts—that administers justice from the national level down to the villages. However, the judiciary finds itself constantly subjected to interference from the executive branch. For example, in one instance in 2001,

This government building is found in the capital city of Asmara.

the president of the High Court was fired for criticizing the government for judicial interference.

SIX REGIONS

Eritrea is divided into six regions, each of which has its own capital. Asmara is the capital city of both the central province and the entire country. Each region is further divided into subregions and towns. While national elections have not been held since 1993, local and regional elections take place on a regular basis, though they are tightly controlled by the PFDJ.

Regional governors are mostly nominated by the president, and their appointment is ratified, or approved, by the National Assembly. A governor oversees a team of local councilors, who are directly elected by the residents of their village or town. Regional elections held in 2002 chose 377 representatives. In local elections in 2004, 12,000 candidates made it to the local councils. Each council manages the daily running of a constituency and looks after the welfare of the residents.

Regional and local administration is often inefficient due to a lack of funds. Many local councils do not function properly because staff members are poorly trained.

SETTING UP A CONSTITUTION

After gaining independence in 1993, the government set up a Constitutional Commission to draft Eritrea's first governmental constitution. To ensure the best possible constitution, the commission sought the views of as many Eritreans as possible, both at home and abroad. Even Eritrean refugees in Sudan were involved in the information-gathering process. The constitution was ratified in May 1997 but has not been fully implemented.

The country's democratic constitution guarantees freedom of expression and equal rights for all Eritreans, regardless of gender, race, or religion. It also authorizes a multiparty system and allows any number of political parties to take part in elections, provided that they are not based on religious or ethnic foundations. Despite this wording, national elections are not held, and only one political party exists.

All Eritreans age 18 and above are entitled to vote in both regional and national elections. However, national elections have been continually postponed since the ratification of the constitution.

DISSENT AND ARREST

With the delay in holding national elections, dissatisfaction started to sweep through some factions of the PFDJ, especially in view of what they considered to be President Afwerki's increasingly autocratic ways. In 2001, several prominent party members publicly called for elections and for the implementation of the constitution. Afwerki's response was to arrest 11 dissidents and hold them without charge. At the same time, the government shut down the independent press and arrested several reporters and editors. Some, including Dawit Isaak, who holds dual Swedish and Eritrean citizenships, were still in jail without having been formally charged as of 2019.

In 2002, the National Assembly decided that the creation of political parties was not important for Eritrea, thus reaffirming the PFDJ as the only legal party in the country. A number of illegal parties and pressure groups operate both within and outside the country.

ENDING CONSCRIPTION

For decades, every Eritrean between the ages of 18 and 40, male or female, was expected to contribute to the country's welfare by performing 18 months of national service. Students who had completed secondary school underwent 6 months of military training at Sawa Military Base. Then, they spent 12 months repairing roads or helping to educate illiterate adults. National service teams constructed dams and wells, repaired roads, terraced hillsides to reduce erosion, and planted millions of tree seedlings. Men and women were also expected to serve 6 months in the military. Until they completed this service, they were not allowed to attend college or get a job. The majority of the time, the 18 months were involuntarily extended to two years or more—many service terms were extended indefinitely.

Although women are often treated as inferior to men in Eritrea, they are still expected to fight as soldiers.

After the peace deal with Ethiopia in 2018, human rights groups hoped that Eritrea's enforced conscription would end. A statement was released in March 2019 asking for an official timeline on "dismantling the compulsory national service." Part of the reason human rights activists have gotten involved is that, in addition to forcing this time served on people, there are multiple rumors that these Eritreans are being mistreated. "Their pay remains inadequate and reports of abuses, including torture, persist," stated Human Rights Watch (HRW) in March 2019. HRW labeled this type of national service "enslavement." Although the government has made promises to disband the national service requirement or stick to the 18-month limit, progress has been slow, and HRW worries that it will not happen.

The enforced conscription has led to more than half a million young people fleeing Eritrea rather than going into the military. Reports indicate

The Eritrean flag has gone through quite an evolution over the last 60-plus years. Its first flag, created in 1952, was light blue, with a wreath of two olive branches surrounding a third upright branch in the middle. It was replaced in 1993, after Eritrea's independence. This flag was designed to represent the Eritrean People's Liberation Front. Made up of three triangles, it had a bright gold star to the left center. The green triangle represented the fertility of the country, while the blue stood for the ocean. The red triangle was for the lives lost in the fight for freedom. The star stood for the rich minerals of the land, while each individual point represented equality, unity, liberty, justice, and prosperity. The current flag is quite similar to that one, but the star has been replaced with the olive branches used in the past. The 30 leaves used in the symbol represent the number of years spent fighting for independence. The president's flag is similar to the new national flag but with the country's national emblem, which features a camel, in the place of the olive wreath.

Eritrea's national crest is a camel encircled by an olive wreath. In Eritrea, the camel is a symbol of the country's success in achieving independence. On the crest, below the camel, the word "Eritrea" is written in three languages, including English.

that thousands leave home every single month. Most go to neighboring Sudan, moving into overcrowded camps that do not have the resources to support them.

WORKING WITH THE WORLD

Eritrea is a member of a number of international organizations, including the UN, the World Health Organization, the International Monetary Fund, and the International Organization for Migration. Eritrea also maintains friendly relations with several European countries—especially its former colonial ruler, Italy—and with the United States.

Relations with the immediate neighbors have been a much bigger struggle, primarily due to territorial disputes. Eritrea normalized relations with Sudan in 2006, but accusations continued to fly between the two neighbors over each other's support for opposition forces in the other country. Meanwhile, competition with Yemen over the Hanish Islands in the Red Sea was resolved with international arbitration in 1998. Also in 1998, the border conflict with

Ethiopia flared into a war, and 10 years later, a military confrontation took place along the border with Djibouti. Accusations flew back and forth around the region, including Eritrean hostility toward Ethiopia for supporting Djibouti. The 2018 peace agreement between Ethiopia and Eritrea eased tensions, as did the peace treaty signed between Eritrea and Djibouti later that year. Omar Mahmood, from the Institute for Security Studies, explains, "Resolving the border concerns paves the way for not just the resumption of Eritrea's relationship with Djibouti, but its wider integration into the Horn of Africa, as this was one of the key lingering disputes preventing that." It is hoped that relations with all neighboring countries will continue to improve in the years ahead.

INTERNET LINKS

https://www.aljazeera.com/news/2018/07/ethiopia-eritrea-peace-leaders-sign-state-war-180710105638000.html
Watch as Ethiopia's and Eritrea's leaders sign the 2018 peace agreement.

https://www.newsweek.com/who-isaias-afwerki-eritreas-enigmatic-dictator-515761
Learn more about Eritrea's president, Isaias Afwerki, and his rise to power.

https://rsf.org/en/eritrea
The organization Reporters Without Borders keeps track of the state of press freedom in countries around the world, including Eritrea.

http://unpan1.un.org/intradoc/groups/public/documents/cafrad/unpan004654.pdf
This PDF shows Eritrea's constitution.

ECONOMY

Eritrean money, called nakfa, is colorful and portrays its people as healthy and happy.

ERITREA'S ECONOMY HAS struggled for decades, and despite the big changes in 2018, it continues to do so. For 30 years, it was gutted by the fight for independence. Then, it was negatively impacted by the border war with Ethiopia that began 1998. Even now, it is still vulnerable and struggling, thanks, in large part, to the government's restrictive policy that keeps most companies under the control of the PFDJ.

Eritrea had no external debt when it became independent, as its debt was absorbed by Ethiopia. However, by 2007, it owed $311 million. By 2016, the number had grown to $870 million.

Inflation has dropped over the past decade, reaching around 9 percent—still somewhat high—in 2018. After falling into negative territory in 2000, the gross domestic product (GDP) growth rate bounced back to reach 5 percent in 2017. GDP is the total value of the goods and services produced in a country within a certain time frame.

FARMING FOOD

Eighty percent of the Eritrean population depends on agriculture for a living, but this sector accounts for less than 12 percent of the GDP. Eritrea is not able to grow enough food to keep its people fed, so it depends

Eritrea's government does not set a minimum wage for private-sector jobs, but the minimum wage for public-sector jobs in 2017 was 360 nakfa per month, or the equivalent of $24. With such low wages, Eritrea is one of the poorest nations in the world.

Two Eritrean farmers work to sift grain by hand.

on importing millions of dollars' worth of products such as wheat, sorghum, pasta, soybean oil, and raw sugar. Poor soil, erratic rainfall, and outdated cultivation methods hamper any attempt to increase agricultural yields. Soil erosion on the central plateau, severely depleted forest resources, and recurrent droughts every three to five years also present major challenges to the industry. Nevertheless, there is great potential for improvement. There is a total of 1.7 million acres (690,000 hectares) of arable land in the country, which accounts for 6.8 percent of Eritrea's total land area.

Before World War II, the Italian colonists set up large irrigated plantations that produced a variety of cash crops, but the war destroyed almost everything, and cultivation is now done mainly by subsistence farmers. These farmers produce food for their own use and a small surplus for trade.

Farmers in the highlands grow several types of traditional grain, such as teff, wheat, millet, barley, and corn. Teff looks like millet and contains yeast, which makes it rise. Being high in protein, complex carbohydrates, and minerals and low in fat, teff is an ideal food and is used to make the national staple bread, *injera* (in-JEHR-uh). The main crops on the lowlands are sorghum, millet, and corn, though this region also supports the growing of vegetables and tropical fruits, such as papayas, bananas, and oranges. Plantations on the escarpment produce cotton, sesame, coffee, rubber, and tobacco.

Pastoralism, or animal husbandry, is an agricultural tradition in Eritrea. Pastoralists focus on raising different types of livestock, including goats, camels, sheep, and cattle, for their milk and meat. Herds are typically moved from one place to another in search of fresh food and water. Two of Eritrea's nomadic tribes, the Beja and the Afar, spend their lives wandering through the nation's lowlands shepherding their animals.

All land in Eritrea is considered state-owned. Individual property is virtually unheard of.

FISHING FOR FOOD

One of Eritrea's most obvious advantages is its long coastline and vast territorial waters. This has helped to create a strong fishing industry. In 2017, fish was the fastest-growing export for the country, increasing more than 174 percent from the previous year. Some of the most popular species to catch and export include tuna, cuttlefish, crabs, parrotfish, oysters, and sea cucumbers. The Red Sea is still under-fished and could potentially provide a major source of revenue for the country.

A number of Eritrean men spend their day at sea fishing for food for their families and to sell at local markets.

With the help of the UN, the Ministry for Marine Resources has put in place a Fisheries Development Project to maximize revenue from offshore fishing and fish processing, while protecting and preserving marine resources through nature reserves. The project funds the purchase of bigger boats and better fishing gear while educating fishermen on modern fishing techniques. Infrastructure such as jetties and boat repair plants have been built in several fishing communities, and a boat factory has been set up in Haleb. Fish processing plants export tons of fish every month to the European market, and in 2019, the nation's stable fish yield was estimated at 80,000 tons (72,574 metric tons) per year.

INDUSTRY AND TRANSPORTATION

Many of the big names in the Eritrean economy originated in the Italian colonial era's period of industrial expansion. Most of these factories were concentrated in Asmara, and they produced food products, beer, tobacco, textiles, and leather goods. Eritrea soon acquired a reputation for producing shoes of good quality. The native workforce at that time learned skills that helped them find jobs abroad when they left their country during the war years.

The Bisha mine has been helpful to Eritrea's economy, but it has also come under scrutiny for human rights violations.

Heavy industry consists of salt and cement plants near Massawa. Another source of revenue is a mine in Bisha that produces metals such as copper, zinc, and gold. Since the Bisha mine opened in 2010, it has brought in more than $755 million for the nation's economy. However, its owner, the Canadian mining company Nevsun, has been accused of forcing people to work in and build the mine, as well as torturing workers. These are serious issues that are still being discussed as of 2019. An additional mineral mine in Asmara is slated to open in early 2020.

The rebuilding of the Massawa—Asmara railroad was one of the most demanding infrastructure projects in the country to date. Originally built by the Italians, the railroad was totally destroyed during the war for independence by Ethiopian soldiers, who used the rails to build trenches. Using the expertise of the original railroad builders and materials salvaged from the abandoned lines and trains, the Eritrean government completed the rebuilding in 2003 at a cost of just 5 percent of what was originally required to build the lines the first time around. With its capacity of 800,000 tons (725,748 metric tons) of freight a year, the railway has boosted the economy while becoming a tourist attraction itself.

UNDER THE GROUND AND IN THE SEA

Much of Eritrea's most valuable resources are found on and under the ground in substantial mineral deposits. Vast salt flats lie like ice-covered lakes in the area around Assab, in Massawa, and in the Kobar Sink in the Danakil Depression. Salt mining is a traditional occupation for Eritreans in the Southern Red Sea region. Miners dislodge slabs of solid salt during the dry season and sell the crude blocks at the closest markets. In addition, deposits of granite, marble, slate, and limestone can be quarried for use in the construction industry.

People traveling on Eritrea's trains enjoy the scenery, especially in the mountains.

Other commercially viable minerals in Eritrea are the metallic ores of gold, silver, copper, zinc, lead, and iron and industrial minerals, such as sulfur, feldspar, gypsum, silica, and potash. The mining industry is strong in Eritrea and accounts for most of the country's output economically. A number of foreign countries have invested in the industry, including China. In late 2019, Australia began exploring a potash project in the Danakil Depression. Potash is used as a fertilizer in many countries. Since potash is found close to the surface, mining it should be simple, but the environment is certain to be a challenge, as it is one of the hottest places on Earth.

The proximity of the oil-rich Arabian Peninsula has raised hopes of finding petroleum in Eritrean territory. Although efforts since the days of Italian rule have been unproductive, surveys have indicated the presence of oil and natural gas deposits in the Red Sea. In the past, President Afwerki has implied that oil has been discovered in great quantities, but the claim has not been followed up with an exploration. Instead, the economic emphasis has remained on mining, but that is rumored to be changing. As more oil has been discovered in nearby areas, the interest in what Eritrea might have has grown. In 2016, Eritrea's Ministry of Energy and Mines announced that the country's Red Sea coast was open for exploration.

AN ECONOMIC IMBALANCE

Eritrea has an extremely unfavorable balance of trade, importing much more than it exports. In 2017, the country exported an estimated $624.3 million in minerals, livestock, textiles, sorghum, food, and small consumer products. However, that same year, it imported almost twice that amount, about $1.1 billion, in machinery, petroleum products, food, and manufactured goods.

Eritrea's largest foreign market is China, which absorbs more than 60 percent of Eritrea's exports. Its second-largest market is South Korea, which accounts for 28 percent of the nation's exports. Eritrea spends a great deal of money on imports from the United Arab Emirates, as well as China, Saudi Arabia, and Italy.

PLANES, TRAINS, AND BUSES

A strategic location on the Red Sea endows Eritrea with the natural potential to be a transportation hub for northeastern Africa. The ports of Massawa

and Assab serve as gateways to many of the neighboring lands. Direct access to an international shipping route extends Eritrea's reach to regional and global markets. Global transportation and communication is also possible from Asmara. There are a total of 13 airports in Eritrea, but only 4 of them have paved runways.

Improving internal transportation and communication networks is a priority for the government. Most of the fixed-line telephones are located in the capital city of Asmara. Less than 1 Eritrean in 100 has a landline. Mobile phones were introduced in 2003, but only 9 of every 100 inhabitants owned one by 2016.

Stretching 190.5 miles (306.4 km) from Massawa to Agordat is the Eritrean railway system. Built in the late 1800s, it was originally used to move military personnel from one location to another, as well as to carry minerals from the mines to the markets. Over the years, it fell into disrepair, until 1996, when retired engineers began to repair it. It was reopened in 2003 for tourists to use. The trip includes more than 30 tunnels and 65 bridges and takes passengers through the highlands to the coastal lowlands.

Eritrea has about 9,940 miles (16,000 km) of roads, but only 10 percent of them are paved. Intercity buses have no fixed timetable and depart only when they are filled. For longer journeys, they stop once or twice along the way for refreshments and visits to the restroom. Taxis are available in Asmara, but

The international airport in Asmara looks clean and modern in the middle of the Eritrean landscape.

CABLEWAY

Construction on the 45-mile (72 km) Asmara-Massawa Cableway was started in 1937 and took two years to complete, requiring 4,300 tons (3,900 metric tons) of cables and other materials. Upon its completion, it was the longest cableway in the world. Powered by eight stations and moving at 5.6 miles (9 km) per hour, its 1,620 trolleys traveled through the air, suspended from the cables. The trolleys could transport 720 tons (653 metric tons) of cargo every day from the coast to the higher elevations of the capital. Bombing in World War II significantly damaged the cableway, putting it out of use. Later, the British sold the scrap materials that were salvageable abroad, mostly to Sudan and Pakistan.

Shown here is a waterfront hotel in Eritrea.

they are not metered, so visitors are encouraged to make sure of the fare before getting in the cab. Rural travel tends to focus on walking or on the use of camels or donkeys.

COME AND STAY

The Eritrean economy is largely based on the concept of self-reliance. In the government's opinion, the country should not accept any handouts from rich countries or nongovernmental organizations. It achieved independence without outside help, and so it believes it can achieve economic security without assistance as well. The leadership also emphasizes resilience, believing that backing away from a challenge is not acceptable. Instead, the people should work even harder to achieve their goals.

Currently not a main industry, tourism is a potential growth area for Eritrea, and visions on how the sector could grow have been in the works for a long time. In 1999, the government established the 2000—2020 Eritrea Tourism Development Plan. This plan has resulted in renovating and extending transportation and infrastructure in the country's most popular cities. A new airport was built in Asmara, and tourist centers were added in the Dahlak Islands. Eritreans hope that these changes will bring more people to their country to visit sites, spend time on beaches, and explore islands.

INTERNET LINKS

https://easyscienceforkids.com/all-about-mining
Understand more about mining at Easy Science for Kids.

http://www.eritrea.be/old/nakfa-history.htm
Read about what some of Eritrea's ancient coins looked like at this website.

http://www.shabait.com/about-eritrea/erina/15824-asmara -massawa-cableway-part-i
This article discusses the history behind building the Asmara-Massawa Cableway.

https://www.youtube.com/watch?v=g5pp3atDN-4
This video examines what the Eritrean currency looks like.

ENVIRONMENT

Where once animals were plentiful in Eritrea, they now have to fight for survival.

5

LOOKING AT THE DRY, DESOLATE, AND barren land of Eritrea today, it can be hard to imagine that in ancient times, the area was known for its wildlife. Nearly every species of African mammal roamed the nation. Then, colonial powers started to lay waste to the country. Today, due to the long border war with Ethiopia, recurrent droughts, and development, the land tells a very different story than it did in ancient times. Many of the animal species are now extinct or find their habitats shrinking rapidly. Humans also struggle to scratch a meager living out of this scorched earth. This fragile environment needs to be healed and preserved, but that is a true challenge. The government has to balance protecting the environment with meeting the needs of its people.

"We fundraised with events and ads and concerts, and we looked for sponsors. Then we used that money to donate solar panels and batteries to families in Eritrea."
　　—Grace Mahary, fashion model and founder of Project Tsehigh, which is dedicated to providing solar power to Eritrea

WEATHER'S IMPACT

Forests cover a small amount of Eritrea's total land area. How much is able to grow in each part of the country depends almost entirely on the weather. For example, the green belt, an area northeast of Asmara, receives more than 39 inches (100 cm) of rain during its two rainy seasons. This means the area is lush and green. At the higher levels, junipers and acacia trees grow, and on the lower levels, shrubs and bushes are found.

The central plateau, on the other hand, has unreliable rainfall and temperatures, so junipers mix with tropical species like African wild olives. The lowlands are quite different from each other. While the southwestern lowland zone has grassland, palm trees, and jujubes (a kind of small date), the northwestern lowland zone only supports semiarid species.

Mangroves cover 29 square miles (75 sq km) and run along 236 miles (380 km) of the Red Sea coast. Mangroves are vital trees in many coastal environments, including Eritrea. The species is protected under multiple international agreements because it plays such an essential role in protecting

For many farmers, finding enough grass to feed their livestock is a daily challenge.

the land from sea-level rises and provides food and habitats for multiple species, such as fish, crabs, and oysters.

FADING FORESTS

Deforestation, or the removal of trees from land to use it for other purposes, is one of the greatest threats to Eritrea's environment. From 30 percent a century ago, forest cover has shrunk to just over 15 percent. Since Italian colonization, large tracts of land have

Much of Eritrea's landscape reflects the damage and destruction of cutting down its trees.

been cleared for agriculture. Today, farmers are still converting forested land into fields for the production of grain. As the population increases, more land is needed to grow food. Unfortunately, yields are low because of poor methods of production and lack of expertise. Moreover, because the traditional land tenure system allows farmers the use of fields for a number of years only, there is no incentive to maintain the quality of the soil, resulting in poor soil condition. At the same time, grasslands suffer from overgrazing, since more cattle are reared for the growing population. To make matters worse, Eritrea has experienced a steady decline in rainfall since the 1940s, leading to long periods of drought.

During the war with Ethiopia, both sides cut down trees. The Eritrean army needed the wood for building trenches as well as for cooking purposes. The Ethiopians, on the other hand, uprooted thousands of trees to destroy the cover they provided for the Eritrean soldiers.

The main cause of deforestation today is the cutting of trees for fuel. In a country where the price of fuel is prohibitively high and electricity does not reach every household, wood-burning stoves are used to cook all meals. Firewood represents almost 70 percent of the total energy consumption of the country, with most of the fuel wood coming from the western lowlands. Substituting dung and crop residues for fuel also causes environmental problems because the nutrients from these alternatives are not going back into the soil, thus causing land degradation.

The Sahara may look just like an endless stretch of sandy desert, but it has been the site of one of the most ambitious environmental actions in the 21st century. The Sahel, a semiarid region at the southern edge of the Sahara, has endured frequent droughts, heavy grazing by animals, and humans cutting down trees for firewood—in short, profound overuse—leaving the land dry and barren.

In 2007, a group of 12 African nations decided that something had to be done to protect and reinvigorate the desert land. They started a tree-planting program called the Great Green Wall of Africa. Participating nations reached from Senegal in the west to Sudan and Eritrea in the east. The plan was to put up a wall of trees to stop the Sahara's supposed spread to the south, into the Sahel. This barrier would do more than stop the sand, however. It would also make the soil more fertile and make it easier to grow food crops.

The Great Green Wall was an ambitious project. It was envisioned to be 9 miles (14.5 km) wide and 4,750 miles (7,644 km) long. The hope was to restore 247 million acres (100 million ha) of land by 2030 and, in the process, create thousands of jobs. However, it wasn't a scientifically supported project, and speculation about its effectiveness grew until new ideas were put forth.

Today, the endeavor has evolved into something more stable. Rather than planting an actual tree wall in the desert—where efforts at forestation have been ineffective since the 1980s—the countries involved are adjusting their planting and farming processes to establish a front line of forests in different locales across the continent. In countries such as Niger and Burkina Faso, farmers have started using older, indigenous planting techniques that seem to be effective in combating desertification and erosion. In Sengal, volunteers planted trees and grass on 494 acres (200 hectares) in the hope of growing sustainable forests. Time will tell if these measures are enough to stem the shifting sands and bring back forests to a dry land.

Ultimately, deforestation leads to soil erosion and desertification. Land degradation in Eritrea has reached an alarming level, resulting in a dramatic decline in agricultural yield levels. However, deforestation is not the only cause of land degradation. Ironically, certain trees have an adverse effect on the environment. The eucalyptus tree, introduced from Australia more than a century ago, is grown extensively in the highlands for firewood. Unfortunately, its long roots cover large areas and consume large amounts of underground water. Cacti behave in the same way, causing the soil to dry up in the long run. The worst culprit is the *temer musa*, which appeared in Eritrea in the early 1990s. Spreading at a fast rate, it absorbs almost all the underground water and exterminates all plants around it.

Efforts have been made by governmental and local groups to rebuild the forests of Eritrea. In 2009, the government partnered with two other organizations to form the Sustainable Land Management (SLM) project. This project called for afforestation, or the process by which many trees are planted in the hope of forming a large, thriving forest in the future. Over the last decade, over 2 million trees have been planted. The project involved 28 villages around Asmara. All benefited from such planting, and other measures have been taken to ensure protection of the environment in which the trees will grow. For example, modern and smokeless cooking stoves have been installed in families' homes.

THE MANZANAR PROJECT

Since the mid-1990s, the village of Hirgigo on the Red Sea has been the site of an almost miraculous regeneration of habitat. Squeezed between barren mountains and the sea, this little desert village is a most unlikely place to witness such rejuvenation. The region is one of the hottest in the world, with temperatures soaring above 104°F (40°C) throughout the year and an average annual rainfall of just 1 inch (2.5 cm).

Started by American biochemist Dr. Gordon Sato in the late 1980s, the Manzanar Project aims to improve the lives of desert coastal communities by using mangroves to increase fish production and combat desertification. Mangroves used to grow along the shore in Hirgigo, but most were cut down for firewood or to build huts. The rest were destroyed by overgrazing by camels. Replacing the mangrove trees prevents coastal erosion, as the strong roots keep the soil from being washed away. The mangrove forest also acts as an ecosystem for fish, crabs, shrimp, and oysters, thus providing food for the village. The trees themselves are a source of food—excess leaves and seeds are fed to sheep and goats—while dry branches are used as firewood.

Today, tall mangrove trees stretch over 4 miles (7 km) of coast. More than a million trees have been planted since the project began. This green band has had a massive impact on the community of about 3,000 people. Many women are employed to plant seeds and collect leaves, whereas the men go out to fish and sell their catch. Not only has the fish population grown in quantity, but also they are bigger in size.

In a region where water is a luxury, using salt water to plant trees provides a lifeline for the village community. Going one step further, Dr. Sato's team has been able to plant mangroves in areas where the trees did not exist previously. To do this, low-cost slow-release fertilizer packs of nitrogen, phosphorus, and iron are planted alongside each seed so that it will receive all the nutrients essential for growth. This project opens up immense possibilities for desert coastal areas where food production is very difficult.

"This is a low-tech solution to hunger and poverty," states Ammanual Yemane, project manager of the nation's Fisheries Ministry. "In these times of food price rises and global warming, it is just what the world needs ... Ours is a small and little-known country, but we have a unique project here that can serve as a model to the world." It is little surprise that mangrove plantations have come to be known as "rain forests" of the sea.

LOSING HABITATS

One of the biggest impacts of deforestation is loss of animal species as their habitats are destroyed. Every type of large game of the East African savanna was present in Eritrea as recently as the mid-20th century. Today, only gazelles, antelopes, leopards, zebras, hyenas, and monkeys can be seen in large numbers. The giraffe, rhinoceros, and hippo no longer roam the country. The Abyssinian wild ass is critically endangered, with fewer than 500 living on the coastal plains. More than 200 species are currently listed as endangered in this nation. One of them is the African elephant. Between 1955 and 2001, there were no sightings at all, and the elephant was thought to have gone extinct within the country. However, in December 2001, a herd of about 30 was spotted near the Gash River. Today, there are about 100 elephants left in Eritrea.

In 1979, sub-Saharan Africa was home to more than 1.3 million elephants. By 2019, that number had dropped to 400,000. Researchers reported that almost 55 African elephants were dying every single day, primarily killed by ivory poachers. In 2014, the leaders of five African countries—Botswana, Chad, Ethiopia, Gabon, and Tanzania—decided something had to be done. They founded the Elephant Protection Initiative (EPI) to help protect elephants and put an end to the ivory trade.

In August 2019, Eritrea became the 20th member to join the EPI. At that time, Miles Geldard, the organization's CEO, stated, "We are delighted that Eritrea has joined the EPI. Elephants have been recorded in Eritrea since Biblical times, and today the elephants of the Gash Setit region, which are believed to migrate between Eritrea and Ethiopia, are a symbol of resilience and hope. We will do our utmost to assist the Eritrean government in their conservation, and in ensuring Eritreans derive benefits from these efforts."

Lions are reported to live in southwestern Gash-Barka region, but the only confirmed sighting was in 2016 in a remote national park in neighboring Ethiopia. The painted hunting dog is extinct, but foxes and jackals are quite plentiful. Baboons live in the highlands, where they need cliffs to sleep. Hares, mongooses, badgers, and aardvarks can be encountered in areas with high human populations.

More than 570 species of birds make their nest in Eritrea, with nearly 20 endemic species. As the country lies on one of the major migration routes into Africa, large numbers of raptors pass through. Within Africa, the white-collared kingfisher is only found in Eritrea. It breeds in the coastal mangrove forests. The Dahlak Islands are important breeding sites for a number of sea and shore birds, including the white-eyed gull, the crab plover, and several terns and boobies. The Socotra cormorant, which also breeds in the southern islands, is a vulnerable species on the International Union for Conservation of Nature (IUCN) Red List of Threatened Species.

Many of the islands in Eritrea are home to a number of bird species.

THE SEA'S DIVERSITY

Famed for its marine diversity, the Red Sea supports the highest degree of native marine species in the world. At least 17 percent of the 1,400 species of fish and 20 percent of the 250 coral species recorded here are found nowhere else on Earth. Eritrea's coastal waters have a favorable climatic condition for reef growth, with warm waters and low rainfall. Here, coral exists mainly as patch reef, extending from the surface to a depth of about 50 feet (15 m). A smaller amount of fringing reef can also be found. Reef formation is stronger around the island coastlines, whereas the reefs along the mainland coastline are less developed mainly due to sedimentation from river runoff. The most pristine reefs occur in the Dahlak Archipelago. Although Eritrean corals have not suffered from any major disaster in the past few decades, the Red Sea marine environment is highly susceptible to pollution, mainly because of its small size and limited oceanographic circulation.

The waters off the coast of Eritrea support a wide variety of marine wildlife, with 600 resident species of fish. The most common reef fish are the colorful surgeonfish, wrasse, snapper, angelfish, and grouper. The whale shark and manta ray also patrol the waters. Four species of whale live in the Red Sea, of which the Bryde's whale and the sperm whale are endangered. Four species of dolphin are also frequently seen in Eritrean waters. Although it is distributed over a wide area, the bottlenose dolphin is a protected species. Fishing communities do consume the meat of dolphins if they are caught accidentally and die in nets. In addition, the skin of the dolphin is used to produce a type of oil, which is valued for its medicinal properties. The dugong, a shy marine mammal also called a "sea cow," finds a very favorable habitat among the sea grasses of the Red Sea. It lives in pairs or small groups in the shallow coastal waters of Eritrea. Worldwide, the dugong has a vulnerable rating from the IUCN, and within Eritrea, the exact population numbers are unknown. Visitors to the waters seldom spot one.

Five of the world's seven sea turtle species breed in Eritrea. They are the hawksbill, olive ridley, loggerhead, leatherback, and green turtle. The mainland coastline, as well as some of the larger islands, provide good nesting grounds for greens, hawksbills, and olive ridleys. All five species are threatened—many

AN AMAZING REDISCOVERY

In April 2019, Eritrea's director of wildlife conservation and development got the shock of his life. While doing a wildlife survey, he spotted a group of 10 gazelles. He suspected that they were a species of gazelle that had not been seen in his country for more than 80 years. He quickly took photographs of the animals and sent them in for verification. He was right! First discovered in 1863, the Eritrean gazelle had not been spotted in the area since the 1930s. Don Church, president of Global Wildlife Conservation, says, "The rediscovery of the Eritrean Gazelle is a great story in part due to the dedication it took to find the species, but also because it gives great hope that other large mammals that have gone undetected may still be hanging on in relatively unexplored areas of our planet."

being endangered or critically endangered. Despite official bans and educational measures, the coastal population still consumes turtle products, mainly eggs and meat. Turtles are also caught in the nets of fish trawlers.

AN INVISIBLE THREAT

Eritrea ranks second behind Angola on the list of African countries most affected by land mines. During the country's long struggle for independence and again when it was at war over its border with Ethiopia, thousands of land mines were laid by both sides. A 2013 report stated that there were still 434 mined areas covering 13 square miles (33.4 sq km). The problem is almost nationwide, with areas in the north of the country and the highlands affected as much as those in the disputed border zone. In the latter region, both antipersonnel and antivehicle mines pose a great danger. Mines were used to defend strongholds around cities and populated areas, military camps and roads, and water sources.

Thousands of people in hundreds of communities are socially and economically affected by mines and unexploded ordnance. Most people at risk are rural inhabitants, nomadic people, internally displaced persons, and refugees. Land mines not only cause physical injury to humans and animals, but they also destroy the environment. More than half of the people who

In the wake of the multiple conflicts between Ethiopia and Eritrea, children are taught about the dangers of land mines, especially in schools in both countries along the border.

are disabled in Eritrea are land mine survivors, making land mines the most pressing cause of physical disability in the country.

The Eritrean government agreed to the Mine Ban Treaty in 2001. Under the terms of the treaty, the country was supposed to have destroyed all antipersonnel mines in mined areas under its jurisdiction or control by February 1, 2012, at the latest. However, in May 2015, the deputy general manager of the Eritrea Demining Agency (EDA) reported "no significant progress" in reducing land mine contamination. Although the EDA stated it would make a stronger effort to improve the situation, it failed to respond to requests for updates in 2016 or 2017. In the meantime, mine risk education continues to be taught to thousands of children and adults in schools and communities. Local populations are taught to recognize land mines and other weapons and to avoid contact with them.

MINING TROUBLE

Eritrean soil is rich in base metals and gold, and exploration activities have confirmed that prospects for the mining industry are excellent. The country is sitting on a potential hoard of several billion pounds of zinc, millions of pounds of copper, and millions of ounces of gold and silver.

Eritrea has several very successful mines, with more being planned. They produce large amounts of metals, as well as potash. The Eritrean government views the mining industry as just what it needs for its struggling economy. It has a financial stake in all mining ventures and so benefits from each new find.

The downside of the mining industry is that it leads to the further degradation of the environment. The open-pit operation in use in Bisha is ecologically harmful as it requires the clearing of large tracts of land and creates pollution. The indigenous population is displaced, and their lifestyle is inexorably changed.

RECOVERY AND REFORESTATION

The Eritrean government has put in place a vast program of environmental recovery, beginning with reforestation of the hillside catchment area. Immediately after independence, a tree-planting campaign encountered great success, especially from students and the army. The Ministry of Agriculture has now turned its attention to the conservation of woodlands and wildlife. A total ban on the cutting of live trees, the hunting or capture of wildlife, and charcoal making is in force. Adapted from an old tradition practiced by the local communities, the government policy of forest closure enables the natural vegetation to regenerate successfully. "Temporary closure" is carried out for a limited period of time, from a few months to a few years. "Permanent closure" creates favorable conditions for vegetation recovery, protects endangered flora and wildlife, controls runoff and loss of arable land by erosion, and increases infiltration for water conservation and for more soil moisture. The Semenawi Bahri National Park (also called Filfil National Park), north of Asmara, is an example of permanent closure.

The other national park in the country is the Dahlak Marine National Park in the Red Sea. The waters around the Dahlak Islands teem with fish and coral. Scuba diving is strictly regulated, and visitors need a permit to enter the area. In 2006, Eritrea announced that it would become the first country in the world to turn its entire coast into an environmentally protected zone. As of 2014, however, no such areas were in place on land or in the waters. That year, the country joined a conservation project that attempted to more concretely step in the direction of protecting species and habitats around the country by setting up systems for managing the conservation of important natural areas.

WIND AND SUN

In addition, there has been a big push in Eritrea to make the most of wind energy and lessen the focus on wood fuel. The United Nations Development Programme has partnered with the Eritrean government to create a wind energy project in the Southern Red Sea region, called the Eritrean Wind Energy Application Project. With a capacity of 750 kilowatts, this wind farm provides power to the port city of Assab. Six other stand-alone wind turbines have been installed in six other cities. This has resulted in providing reliable energy to more than 35,000 people, as well as to schools, heath centers, and small businesses.

Along with wind energy, Eritrea has explored the effectiveness of solar energy. In 2013, more than 100 solar panels were installed on the roof of the UN office in Asmara. The installation provided enough energy to power the office for eight hours a day. Its success has been inspiring. "This has opened the eyes of the Government," stated Christine Umutoni, the UN resident coordinator in Eritrea. "They are now [starting to] power their streets through solar energy." Another important group is Project Tsehigh. Started in Eritrea, its mission is to promote renewable energy sources to communities and install them in areas most in need. Its first successful endeavor involved installing solar panels in villages. With visions like this, Eritrea is on its way to being a model promoter of renewable energy.

Exploring alternative methods of energy, such as wind power, may be the key to helping the people of Eritrea finally have the electricity they need.

INTERNET LINKS

https://www.awea.org/wind-101/basics-of-wind-energy
Find out more about wind energy at the American Wind Energy Association's website.

https://www.greatgreenwall.org/about-great-green-wall
For information on the Great Green Wall in Africa, check out this film.

https://www.nrel.gov/research/re-solar.html
Explore solar energy at the National Renewable Energy Laboratory's website.

https://www.projecttsehigh.com
This website provides key information about Project Tsehigh, including its origins, goals, and current successes.

ERITREANS

The people of Eritrea must share what
limited resources their country offers.

6

W ITH A POPULATION OF JUST under 6 million, Eritrea has about as many people in its country as the United States has in the states of Maryland or Missouri. For years, the population has struggled to grow because so many people have fled the area, most of them teenage men and women hoping to escape serving in the military. Until 2018, leaving the country without governmental permission was not allowed, and people who did so were punished with fines, prison time, or even death. This made fleeing Eritrea a dangerous decision.

Despite the country's "shoot to kill" policy toward leaving, thousands of people left Eritrea during the 1960s and 1970s. Most of them took refuge in nearby Sudan and Saudi Arabia, as well as in Israel, Europe, and North America. Many settled in California and Minnesota. When Ethiopia and Eritrea's border war ended in 2018, there was great hope that many refugees could come home again. However, decades of mistrust are hard to overcome. "I would love to go [back to Eritrea] with the whole family," Mohammed Lumumba Ibrahim, an Eritrean man who had been living in Germany for 45 years, told the Associated Press after peace was announced. "But I need to make sure myself that we have peace, that

Eritrea's population growth rate is only 0.89 percent a year. Almost 40 percent of the population is under the age of 15, and the average life span is only about 65 years.

there is no war so that I can take my children and show them their fatherland." Despite the thaw in relations with Ethiopia, Eritreans continue to leave because of a lack of political, religious, or social freedom, while others recognize that there is little opportunity for financial security in their homeland.

MAIN ETHNIC GROUPS

The millions of people who still call Eritrea home are diverse and represent a wide variety of languages, cultures, and religions. The main ethnic groups inhabit different parts of the country, but they live in relative unity. Ethnic friction is thus almost nonexistent, and the constitution allows no discrimination against any group. Today, Eritreans show solidarity in their desire to develop their country.

THE TIGRINYA   The Tigrinya make up more than half of Eritrea's entire population, making them the largest of the ethnic groups. Living in the southern

Many ethnic groups make up Eritrea's population. They all have unique traditions, like wearing jewelry, as this woman does.

highlands, the people speak Tigrinya, and most are Christian. As the descendants of early Semitic settlers in the Horn of Africa, the Tigrinya are related to the Sabaean people who claim to be descended from the biblical Queen of Sheba. One of their historical achievements was setting up the ancient empire of Aksum. The Eritrean Tigrinya people share this ancient heritage with the 4 million inhabitants of the Ethiopian region of Tigray.

The Tigrinya are a group of hardworking people whose determination contributed significantly to their country's attainment of freedom. Today, they are helping to build Eritrea with the same perseverance. Their spirit of sacrifice is also noteworthy, and they are likely to go hungry and offer their food to others who need it more.

The Tigrinya people are mostly farmers cultivating vegetables and grain in the temperate highlands. Drinking coffee constitutes an important part of their social life, and the women have a strong penchant for jewelry. The Tigrinya people also have a rich heritage in music, featuring drums and string instruments.

The Tigre people dress in white to help deflect the heat of their homeland.

THE TIGRE About one-third of Eritreans are from the Tigre ethnic group, and they are descendants of ancient Egyptians. Today, many are Muslims leading nomadic lifestyles. They roam the northern highlands and eastern and western lowlands with their herds of goats, sheep, cattle, and camels. Some of the Tigre are farmers who cultivate corn, wheat, barley, and legumes. They live in round huts with cone-shaped roofs and tend to have large families.

THE AFAR Members of the Afar tribe live on the southern desert plains of the country. They are also known as the Danakil, after the region in which they live, but this term offends them. They claim their ancestry in the biblical figure Noah and are a proud and strong people known for being ferocious warriors. Men are commonly not allowed to get married until they have killed someone in battle.

TIGRE MARRIAGE PRACTICE

Many Tigre practices are rooted in tradition. One tradition involves marriage to settle disputes between fighting families. It sometimes happens that a Tigre family offers a daughter in marriage to a man from another Tigre family to resolve a disagreement between the two families that would otherwise end in bloodshed. Marrying often quells any ill feelings, as families take their bonds seriously. In Tigre tradition, marriage is the most important relationship humans can have with each other. Parents often have a say in their child's mate, and arranged marriages sometimes happen. Additionally, much negotiation occurs between the two families prior to a man and a woman marrying. While most Tigre are Muslims, influences from Christianity have also had an impact on Tigre marriages in recent times.

Most Afar are Muslims. They are divided into two subgroups. The "red ones" (as translated from their language) are the powerful nobles living along the coast, while the "white ones" are the commoners living in the mountains and in the Danakil Depression.

Afar huts are put up and taken down quickly. They often have room only for one bed.

The Afar build oval-shaped huts from palm mats and set up camps surrounded by thorn barricades to protect them from wild animals and enemy tribes. Most of the Afar are nomads who herd sheep, goats, cattle, and camels. Some of the Afar have portable huts that they pack up and carry on their backs to their next location. The size of their herds indicates their wealth. Some of the Afar near the Red Sea coast make their living as fishermen as well. The Afar have traditionally traveled beyond Eritrea into Ethiopian and Djiboutian territory, where more of their population lives.

Rashaida women often cover everything but their eyes and arms.

THE BEJA The Beja consider themselves descendants of Noah's grandson Cush. Scattered across the desert regions of Eritrea, Egypt, and Sudan, they are the largest non-Arabic ethnic group between the Nile River and the Red Sea. They have lived in the region for more than 4,000 years and were a powerful people in ancient times. Approximately 200,000 Beja inhabit approximately 20,000 square miles (51,800 sq km) in the western plain in Eritrea. Thousands of Eritrean Beja were driven into Sudan during the war.

There are two Beja tribes in Eritrea: the Hedareb and the Beni-Amer. These tribes are made up of clans varying in size from 1 to 12 families. The Hedareb live in the far north of the country and manifest a strong Arab influence. The Beni-Amer have developed a social system that resembles a caste system and that the government strongly discourages.

With small, strong, and wiry frames, today's Beja are seminomadic shepherds who live in portable tents built by the women. They are Muslims and are often also fluent in Arabic and Tigre. Male children are highly favored among young Beja couples.

SMALLER ETHNIC GROUPS

Together the Nera, Kunama, Bilen, Saho, and Rashaida make up about 12 percent of the Eritrean population. Many minority groups are Muslim. They live in most parts of the country, except in the central highlands. The Nera and Kunama live in the western lowlands. The Bilen are mostly pastoralists who live in the northern highlands, mainly around Keren. The Saho reside on the coastal plain south of Massawa, quite close to the Afar. The Rashaida roam the northern hills as true nomads. A small group of Nigerians lives near Teseney. Their ancestors settled there on the way to or from the Muslim holy city of Mecca in Saudi Arabia. Ethiopians, mostly of Tigrinya heritage, form a small and dwindling minority in Eritrea's ethnic mosaic.

THE ROLES AND RIGHTS OF ERITREAN WOMEN

In Eritrea, being a soldier is not a position reserved for men. Of the 65,000 fighters killed during Eritrea's fight for independence from Ethiopia, for example, one-third were women. Women made up 35 percent of the 95,000-strong EPLF army. Many fought on the front lines during the liberation war, while those who stayed in the villages took over the jobs and roles of the men who had left to fight. This participation was not due, however, to gender equality. Instead, it was due to a severe lack of Eritrean able-bodied fighters.

After returning from the war, Eritrean women were often ostracized. Some were considered too masculine and thus unmarriageable when they got back to their native villages. Their independence and modern ways clashed with the traditional rural lifestyle.

Even today, many village families consider their daughters home laborers and keep them out of school. Although women head more than half of households in some areas, they are often barred from agricultural activities because cultural norms prevent them from farming. Gender equality is enshrined in the constitution, but in reality, women often have a lower status both in the home and in the community. In addition, Muslim women are governed by sharia law, which does not give them much protection. Violence against women is widespread, particularly domestic violence, sexual harassment, and sexual abuse.

Eritrean perceptions of women are slowly changing with the example of female pioneers. Tirhas Iyassu, one of the best female painters in the country, paints images of men looking after children or cooking to promote gender equality. Likewise, women in government, such as Fozia Hashim and Amina Nurhussein, are also inspiring others. The National Union of Eritrean Women is a semi-autonomous nongovernmental organization dedicated to improving the status of Eritrean women. With an ever-growing membership, the group aims to enhance the role of women by raising their political consciousness through literacy campaigns, credit programs, English language lessons, and other skills training. In 2017, they partnered with the United Nations Development Programme on a gender equality campaign.

The Eritrean government recognizes the role of women in national development and guarantees 30 percent of seats in national and regional elections to women, though this percentage has not been achieved in the legislature. President Afwerki has appointed six female ministers in his cabinet, and there are women holding other senior government positions as well.

AWAY FROM HOME

The diaspora is a very important concept to Eritreans. It refers to the many thousands of Eritreans who live outside their home country. Many escaped during the long war for independence from Ethiopia, while others have fled more recently. The Eritrean diaspora is clustered in a variety of countries, both nearby and faraway. For example, about 170,000 Eritreans were living in Ethiopia, 26,000 in Israel, 70,000 in Germany, and 34,000 in the United States as of 2018, while others were living elsewhere in Africa, Europe, or even Australia. Virtually everyone in Eritrea knows someone living outside the country. Although members of the diaspora may have decided to settle permanently in their host countries, many still consider themselves Eritrean and raise their children with an Eritrean cultural awareness.

After liberation, many among the diaspora returned to Eritrea to help in its recovery, while others decided to stay in their host countries and help their home country in an indirect way. The latter regularly send money back to Eritrea, contributing substantially to the country's annual revenue. These funds, called remittances, have formed a large and stable flow of income for many. Today, in large part due to the end of the border war, many Eritreans who left the country as young children have come back as tourists to visit aged relatives and commune with the country of their birth.

CHANGES FOR REFUGEES

During the liberation war, approximately 750,000 Eritreans left the country. Half a million went to neighboring Sudan, 75,000 went to the Middle East, and 25,000 went to Europe and the United States. Most had to battle inhumane conditions in order to reach safety. Some traveled at night on camels or on foot. Others sent their children away to protect them from conscription into the military.

The refugees in Sudan lived in overcrowded camps with very few amenities. Life there was harsh, but far better than in Eritrea. In the camps in Sudan, each family had a hut with a little land to cultivate. The refugees organized their own communities, running schools for their children and rearing animals and crops for food. They earned a salary if they held a job inside or outside the camps. The women formed self-help groups to make handicrafts, which they sold for money. Some of the refugees found sponsors to pay for their migration to the West.

When the EPLF liberated most of the country in 1989, Eritrean refugees began returning home by the thousands. The Commission for Eritrean Refugee Affairs managed the repatriation process and reintegrated the returnees into Eritrean society. Between 1989 and 1992, more than 80,000 refugees returned to Eritrea, with 80 percent coming from Sudan. This sudden influx was a strain on the new country. Housing and social services were overstretched. There were not enough work opportunities for all the returnees. The government instituted a plan to educate former refugees to help them get a job or start a business. Those with good business plans applied for low-interest loans from the government to finance their start-up companies.

Nearly 20 years after independence, the refugee problem was still not completely resolved. More than 100,000 Eritreans were still awaiting repatriation from camps in Sudan, and thousands were leaving the country to avoid conscription and escape the repressive regime of President Afwerki.

In 2018, after Ethiopia and Eritrea reopened their borders, rules temporarily changed. People could come and go without permits or passports. They did not have to let anyone know where they were going or when they would be back. This change made it easy for people to flee the country. The Ethiopian government reported that the number of Eritreans entering their country had increased fourfold. Thousands of people, primarily unaccompanied minors, came in looking for asylum, putting a huge burden on an already taxed nation. In December 2018, Eritrea began placing tighter restrictions on the border again, though such restrictions did not stop refugees in the past.

While some Eritreans remain in Ethiopia, many move on to Europe or North America in search of a better life. As one Ethiopian businesswoman put it, "I don't think there is any way back now for the Eritrean government. Eritreans are experiencing freedom, socializing, and business—the genie is out of the bottle."

INTERNET LINKS

http://theconversation.com/i-asked-young-eritreans-why-they -risk-migration-this-is-what-they-told-me-119324
Read about why some young Eritreans are not willing to stay in their homeland in this interview from the *Conversation*.

https://www.everyculture.com/Cr-Ga/Eritrea.html
Learn more about the Eritrean culture and gender roles from Countries and Their Cultures.

https://www.undp.org/content/dam/eritrea/docs/ WomenEmpowerment/UNDP%20NUEW%20Publication.pdf
Find out more about the National Union of Eritrean Women by reading this report, called "10 Years: Women in Eritrea."

LIFESTYLE

Many Eritreans spend their days walking long distances to get water or other resources for their family.

7

STEPPING INTO MUCH OF ERITREA IS like stepping back in time. Many of the people living there lead lifestyles that, despite the passage of years and significant alterations in government policies, have changed very little. Nomadic tribes are still on the move, following ancient customs and traditions as they search for another rare green patch of grass or a puddle of precious rainwater to keep their livestock alive. Rural farmers spend their days trying to keep crops growing in an increasingly hostile environment and with meager resources. Urban areas have experienced massive reconstruction, but even the large cities of Asmara and Massawa retain an Old World atmosphere with their well-preserved but aging buildings.

"People will either learn the easy way or the hard way. If you aspire to become someone in this society with a good quality of life, you work for it. You don't get it for free. It's as simple as that."
—President Afwerki

In 2007, international organizations and charities such as the United Nations and the World Bank reached out to Eritrea, offering foreign aid, including food, infrastructure loans, and grants. They were all turned down. President Afwerki emphasized the need for self-reliance, stating, "We need this country to stand on its two feet." Even though Eritrea was one of the poorest nations in the world, Afwerki shunned aid, believing that those countries that accepted help were "crippled societies." He added, "You can't keep these people living on handouts because that doesn't change their lives." More than a decade later, Eritrea is still struggling, and the president is still intent on self-reliance. In 2016, Afwerki reluctantly accepted money from the European Development Fund to focus on improving the country's agricultural infrastructure and providing solar energy to some of its most rural areas.

SHRINKING FAMILIES

Eritrean families tend to be slightly larger than Western ones, with the average mother bearing three or four children in her lifetime. Despite this, overall population growth is low in Eritrea. This is largely due to the fact that not all mothers survive childbirth. In the United States, 14 women in 100,000 die in childbirth, but in Eritrea, it is 480 per 100,000. This is coupled with the fact that the country's infant mortality rate is eight times that of the United States. In 2009, the average family had five or more children, but an increased use of birth control has brought that number down.

In the past, the father acted as head of the household and was responsible for earning the money. However, as gender roles have slowly become slightly more equal, women are working outside the home quite often as well. Family chores are shared, although it is still the mother and daughters who are relied on for making meals, cleaning, and doing physical jobs like tending a vegetable garden or bringing home water from the closest well.

Most Eritrean parents tell their children traditional stories handed down from one generation to another. Throughout the nation, there is an attitude that every child is everyone's child. Parenting is often looked on as a communal experience, with relatives and neighbors often stepping in to help nurture little ones.

Many children in Eritrea became orphans when they lost both of their parents in the liberation war. The orphanage system still continues today. The majority of orphans are placed in orphanages until the age of 6. There they are provided with food, shelter, health care, clothing, and education. There is a strong emphasis on love, protection, and affection in these places. Adoption is not common, although older parents or volunteers sometimes step in. Visitors come to the orphanages frequently, bringing gifts and staying long enough to cuddle, read to, and play with the children. At age 6, the children move on to group homes, where they are taught family values, norms, and lessons.

In Eritrea, 60 percent of the people are under the age of 25. While young people often enjoy their freedom and keep busy with hobbies and sports, the majority are married and have their first babies by age 21.

Family is important in Eritrea, but there is little time for leisure and play.

RURAL LIFE

The number of Eritreans living in the countryside has been dropping dramatically over the last decade. In 2004, it was almost 82 percent, but by 2017 it was down to 60 percent.

Many of the families living in rural areas build small huts out of stones, clay, and palm leaves. These can last up to 10 years if the palm is of good quality. On average, it takes four men to build a hut in one day. The shape of the hut and the materials used vary slightly according to the location, lifestyle, and heritage of the tribe. A Nera village, for example, looks like a colony of beehives, as the roofs of the huts reach to the ground. Each Nera family has three huts: one for males, one for females, and one used as a kitchen.

Rural life is a slow-paced life, but not an easy one. The people work hard to grow adequate amounts of grain and vegetables, and to raise enough sheep and cattle to feed themselves. Periodic droughts and famines bring great suffering. Still, there are occasions to celebrate, such as weddings and major festivals, when the whole village comes together in ritualistic ceremonies.

Villages in Eritrea's countryside are often quite simple.

TIFFANY HADDISH

Tiffany Haddish is a comedian and actress with Eritrean roots. Her father is from Eritrea, and the family is proud of its heritage.

At the Oscars in 2018, Haddish wore a particularly detailed dress that got a great deal of attention from reporters. The black, gold, and white floor-length zuria *gown was more than beautiful; it was a tribute to her father. "He said that … if I ever end up at the Oscars, to honor my people," she stated. Her gown's cape was known as a* kaba.

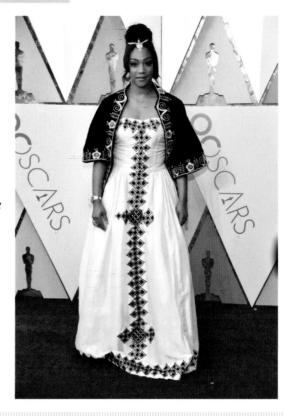

CLOTHING CHOICES

Many Eritrean women dress in long, flowing dresses known as *habesha kemis* or *zurias*. These dresses are usually in gray, white, or beige and are often made of cotton strips woven together. A light shawl, or *kaba*, drapes around their shoulders. Many Tigrinya women wear their traditional dress to festival celebrations and at their wedding. This long, white gown is embellished with golden embroidery around the cuffs and down the front.

Gold sandals are the traditional feminine footwear, while gold jewelry forms a major part of the complete attire. Eritrean women love jewelry. Their earrings, necklaces, rings, armbands, and bracelets used to be made of silver or wood, but the preferred material is gold. Decorative tattoos are very popular in the villages. Some women still tattoo their gums using thorns dipped in charcoal dye and burnt oil to make their teeth appear whiter. It is a painful procedure that is slowly losing its popularity. The traditional hairstyle is called *quno* (KOO-noh). Fine braids of hair stick close to the scalp and spray out from the nape like a giant fan.

Men living in rural areas, especially in the hottest regions, wear the *djellabia* (JEL-lah-bay-ah), a loose, long-sleeved robe made of white or light-colored cotton, over loose cotton trousers. They walk in leather sandals or rubber slippers. Muslim men complete the outfit with a head covering. Men on the coast walk bare-chested, with a sarong—a large piece of cloth—wrapped around them from the waist down. The Beja and Rashaida nomad traders traditionally make their clothes from animal skins, but most now use commercially manufactured fabrics. Eritrean boys mostly wear shorts and T-shirts, while girls wear little dresses, sometimes with a scarf. People in the cities, especially in Asmara, generally wear Western-style dress—that is, shirts or T-shirts and pants for men, and skirts and blouses for women.

CITY LIFE

Homes in urban Eritrea tend to be small, made up of a living room, bedroom, kitchen, and bathroom. Most houses in the larger cities have electricity and running water. In recent years, apartment blocks have sprung up in Asmara. With two or three bedrooms, these new living spaces are considered modern and affluent.

In many households, both parents work while the children go to school. If the mother does not have a formal occupation, she keeps herself busy with church or other voluntary activities. The children are free to play outdoors after school, and they can do so safely, even at night, thanks to a relatively low crime rate.

Friends and neighbors often meet in bars and cafés to chat and to have coffee. A favorite pastime is to stroll along the street in the early evening. Most people in the cities even prefer to walk to and from work rather than ride the buses and horse-drawn carts that run through the towns.

A DAY AT WORK

According to government regulations made more than 20 years ago, all civil servants have to work about 45 hours a week. From Monday to Friday, office hours are from 7:00 a.m. to 12:00 p.m., when there is break for lunch, and then from 2:00 p.m. to 6:00 p.m. On Fridays, the lunch break starts half an hour earlier so that Muslim workers have time to go to the mosque for their weekly devotions. Some enterprises in the private sector still stick to the old system, working from 8:00 a.m. to 5:00 p.m. from Monday to Friday, and half a day on Saturday.

There are no fixed working hours in the countryside, where the time it takes shepherds and farmers to perform their tasks depends on the season and on the condition of their animals and crops.

GOING TO SCHOOL

Almost 74 percent of adult Eritreans are literate, an improvement over just a few years ago. Children are required to be in school from ages 7 to 14; however, the majority of children, male and female, only attend five years of formal schooling. Girls in the rural areas are less likely to go to school than boys.

Children in the lower grades study in their native languages. They gradually absorb Tigrinya, Arabic, and foreign languages, especially English, as they advance to higher levels. Children in the seventh grade and above take all their subjects in English, a legacy of the British protectorate years.

The government is continually taking measures to improve the country's education system. However, for many, the final year of high school remains carried out at the Sawa military training school. Teachers are required to attend summer courses to upgrade their skills, and more schools, including boarding schools, have been built. The Eritrean Institute of Technology is complemented by five colleges of higher education scattered in different parts of Eritrea. Adult education also takes place in vocational training centers located in various towns.

STAYING HEALTHY

Chronic drought and decades of war have taken a toll on the health of Eritreans. Land mines from the war tear off the limbs of anyone who steps in the wrong spot. Lack of adequate food creates malnutrition and stunts the growth of children. Major infectious diseases such as hepatitis, typhoid fever, bacterial diarrhea, malaria, and dengue fever affect both children and adults.

Water is already a scarce resource in Eritrea, and what is available has a high risk of being contaminated and causing serious illness. Approximately 42 percent of all Eritreans live without access to improved drinking water and must rely on polluted water for their drinking or cooking needs. In addition, as much as 85 percent of the nation's residents deal with unimproved sanitation, from improper to nonexistent toilet facilities. Multiple nonprofit groups are working on a regular basis with the Eritrean people to supply clean toileting options, plus education to thousands on proper hand-washing techniques. Along with these efforts, these organizations are also working with the government to upgrade water supply systems and wells, including installing systems that run on solar power.

A network of clinics and small hospitals provides medical care around the country. More than half of the population lives within a few miles of a health facility. Asmara has eleven hospitals, with nine health centers and more than a dozen pharmacies. The Ministry of Health operates a National Blood Transfusion Center in Asmara. Planned Parenthood and the Red Cross have formed local chapters in Eritrea to attend to the population's health needs.

HELP FROM CHINA

Since 1997, China has sent more than 200 doctors and other health-care workers to help the people of Eritrea. At the end of August 2019, a Chinese team of 18 medical providers left the country after being there for more than a year. They worked throughout a number of the hospitals in Eritrea, providing free services, treatments, and diagnoses to thousands of people. They took X-rays, performed surgeries, and even taught traditional Chinese acupuncture to local medical personnel. In addition, China has provided many scholarships and training programs to Eritreans in order to share medical knowledge. In 2019, the Ministry of Information stated, "Eritrea is grateful to the professionalism and outstanding services provided by the Chinese medical team."

Eritreans have had to deal with incredible amounts of hardship during their lifetimes. From political unrest and border wars to the ramifications of climate change, they have had to work hard and focus on enduring. Their strength and determination is clear as they improve much of their country—and recognize that they still have a long way to go.

INTERNET LINKS

http://www.eritrea-chat.com/traditional-house-construction-in-eritrea
This brief movie in English explores Eritrea's traditional way of house construction.

https://www.eritreadigest.com/a-day-in-the-life-of-sawa-high-school-students
In this story, two students discuss their experiences of Sawa, the military training camp where Eritreans spend their final year of high school.

https://www.nwaea.org/media/cms/Eritreas_brochure_AEC19835CFCFD.pdf
This PDF is a brochure about Eritrea's culture.

http://www.shabait.com/about-eritrea/history-a-culture/1385-constructing-houses-among-the-tigre-ethnic-group
See photos and read about how the Tigre people build their houses at this website from the Ministry of Information.

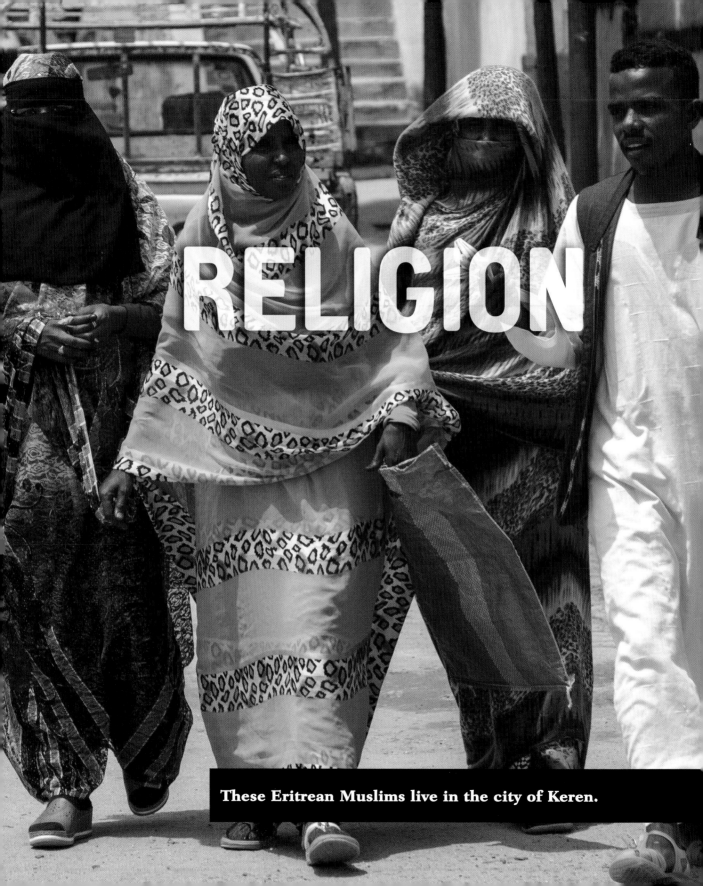

RELIGION

These Eritrean Muslims live in the city of Keren.

8

I N ERITREA, YOU ARE FORTUNATE IF you belong to one of the four permitted religions: Orthodox Christian, Sunni Muslim, Roman Catholic, or Protestant. The nation's constitution guarantees freedom of religion, but a 2002 government decree limited that freedom to only these four belief systems. Anyone who followed another religion was expected to register with the Eritrean government. This has led to news-making incidents of religious persecution.

Eritrea was one of the first countries to adopt Christianity during the fourth century CE. The first converts were along the coast, and then the religion spread to the plateau region. Islam arrived in the country a few hundred years later. Since then, these two faiths have been the most prevalent and supported religions in Eritrea.

FOLLOWERS OF ISLAM

Eritrean Muslims belong to the Sunni branch of Islam. Every Friday, Muslims go to their closest mosque to worship. In Asmara, many flock to the Khulafa el-Rashidin Mosque. Built in 1937, the mosque's minaret reaches so high into the sky, it can be seen from anywhere in the city. The

Many mosques are topped by towers known as minarets.

beautiful building features platforms, balconies, and columns. Each Friday, it overflows with devotees, who spill into the street and kneel on their prayer mats, oblivious to the city traffic.

Religious observance is much simpler in the rural areas. The mosques in Muslim villages do not look much different from the huts. Although most rural Muslims dress in the Arabic style, only Rashaida women cover their faces.

Apart from the Afar, most Muslims in Eritrea do not spend much time studying the Quran, the Islamic holy book. They practice a folk version of the faith, following only some Islamic observances and retaining their pagan beliefs and customs. Most do not eat pork, but the same abstinence does not apply to liquor, which is also prohibited in Islam. Some ethnic groups practice polygamy, or being married to more than one person, which Islam allows.

Muslims are well represented in all the towns in Eritrea, where they have made their mark in trade. The roots of their religion lie in some Dahlak

Islanders, who converted to the faith in the 8th century CE. By the early 10th century, Massawa, too, had Muslim residents. However, it was not until the 16th century that Islam moved farther inland. Two factors contributed to this spread: the expansion of the Turkish Ottoman Empire into Eritrea and the forced conversions of thousands of Christians by Ahmed Gragn, the sultan of Harar. Although Islam never displaced Christianity from the highlands, it continues to dominate the lowlands of Eritrea.

A BRANCH OF CHRISTIANITY

Orthodox Christians in Eritrea were once part of the Ethiopian Orthodox Church, but they established their own branch of the church in the 1990s. The majority of Christians in Eritrea belong to the Eritrean Orthodox Church. Eritrean Orthodox Christianity has its origins in the Syrian Orthodox religion of the fourth century CE and is also closely tied to the church in Egypt. It displays some Jewish influences in the celebration of certain festivals, such as Meskel and Kidus Yohannes (new year). Orthodox Christians in rural Eritrea also observe the Sabbath, the rest day, from Friday night to Saturday night. However, the slaughtering of animals during religious holidays is a remnant of paganism.

The Orthodox Church is very well established in Eritrea, and church activities form a significant part of daily Christian life. A prominent symbol in the Orthodox Church is the Ark of the Covenant, which contains God's Ten Commandments, according to the Bible. The section of the church holding this symbol is not open to anyone but the church's priests. Each church is named after a saint, and celebrations are held each month to honor that saint. In the congregation, men stand on one side and women on the other. There are few chairs or pews. Instead, worshippers stand or kneel during the two-hour services.

During Christian festivals, such as Easter and Christmas, Eritrean Orthodox priests wear colorful and ornate robes and lead processions of devotees through the streets. In the past, services were conducted in Geez, the ancient language of the Aksumite Kingdom, but today most are conducted in the Tigrinya

Like the buildings surrounding it, the Debre Bizen Monastery is made primarily of stone.

language. Emotions run high during church services. Devotees embrace the walls of the church and kiss the ground.

Orthodox churches are usually built on a hill. The Debre Bizen Monastery sits on a plateau at 8,040 feet (2,450 m). It was founded by Abuna Filipos, who began his monastic life in 1361. The monastery survived Somali and Ethiopian invasions and holds 1,000 manuscripts written in Geez. The most important building for Eritrean Orthodox Christians is the Enda Mariam Church in Asmara. Built during the Italian colonial period, it combines Italian and Ethiopian religious styles. Its twin towers are useful landmarks, and its interior is adorned with interesting murals.

The Eritrean and Ethiopian Orthodox Churches have traditionally had their own calendar. Each month has 30 days, and the extra days left at the end of the year make up a short 13th month. This calendar was used during the Ethiopian occupation of Eritrea. After independence, however, the Eritrean government replaced it with the Gregorian calendar used by most of the rest of the world.

PERSECUTION

In 2016, a United Nations human rights commission declared that Eritrea was guilty of "crimes against humanity" due to its repressive tactics, including persecution of religious minorities, journalists, and politicians. Many journalists, government officials, and politicians have disappeared since 2001 following criticism of President Afwerki. As of September 2019, they had not been seen or heard from since their detainment. A call for their immediate release was put forward by Amnesty International in late 2019. However, it is unclear if any steps will be taken by the Eritrean government to do as this group wishes.

This protest image shows a re-creation of one of the shipping containers used to hold journalists, religious minorities, and other prisoners in Eritrea.

In 2017, the Human Rights Council backed up the UN report that labeled the country as one committing crimes against humanity, stating that Eritrea was punishing those who had attempted to "exercise the right to freedom of religion, or freedom of opinion and expression." The report stated that at least 3,000 Eritreans were being forcibly imprisoned. Of those people known to have been arrested, some are kept in conventional prisons, while others are kept in shipping containers in inhumane and dangerous conditions for months to years. The Eritrean government has done little to reform itself in regard to human rights, despite joining the United Nations Human Rights Council and being the subject of several United Nations investigations and mandates.

In July 2018, following the Ethiopia-Eritrea border truce, 35 Christian prisoners from sects other than those approved of by the government were released, to much fanfare. Reverend Abraham Hailu, a Roman Catholic priest from Eritrea, welcomed the release of these prisoners, saying, "We see hope. With this agreement, we hope Eritrea will … release more of its prisoners."

A RELIGIOUS LATECOMER

Shown here is a Catholic cathedral in Eritrea.

A latecomer in Eritrea, Roman Catholicism draws its followers from the Tigrinya and Kunama ethnic groups. The Roman Catholic Church has also attracted more converts in the towns, with its promise of higher education. The first Roman Catholic missionaries were Portuguese priests, who arrived in the 16th century. Their interest in Eritrea was political as much as religious. While trying to convert the population, they also helped the Abyssinians fight the invading Turks.

It was also through a missionary that Italy managed to get a foothold in Eritrea. One of the first Italians in the country was Father Giuseppe Sapeto, who established a mission in Adwa and helped the Italian government purchase land in Eritrea. With the setting up of the Italian colony in 1890, more Eritreans became Catholics.

Catholics in Eritrea are very devout and devote much time to church activities. Services are held weekly on Saturday and Sunday, and it is the same for the Eritrean Orthodox Church. Conducted in Italian or Latin as well as in local languages, services are joyful occasions, full of song and praise.

The Catholic cathedral on Liberation Avenue in Asmara was originally drafted by Italian architect Oreste Scanavini and later redesigned by Mario Mazzetti. Work on the cathedral was finished in 1922. It provides a beautiful view of the city from the top.

In contrast with Muslim graves, which are much simpler in design, Catholic and Orthodox graves are richly decorated with crosses and other sculptures. Catholic homes typically display a large amount of religious imagery, such as crucifixes and pictures of saints.

SHAMANS AND AMULETS

Many Eritreans believe that evil spirits can take animal form to plague human beings with sickness and accidents. For example, the Tigre fear the evil spirit

Zar, which they believe possesses people, sometimes driving them to their deaths. Only a shaman can enter into a trance and communicate with the spirits to exorcise demons and cure diseases. To protect themselves from spirits, believers in animism wear amulets, which sometimes contain verses of the Quran.

Various other ethnic groups also have their own slants on animism. To the Afar, for example, trees and groves, as well as the dead, have special powers, and they hold an annual "feast of the dead" to appease their spirits. The Beja believe that some people have the power to curse others by giving them the "evil eye." The Nera and Kunama believe in a supernatural being in heaven called Ana, whom they pray to for blessings on their harvests.

Despite promises of freedom and acceptance in Eritrea's constitution, those practicing any religion beyond those in the 2002 governmental policy have been at serious risk. Many find it difficult to cheer for the release of a handful of religious prisoners when thousands are still incarcerated simply for having a different set of beliefs. It is one of Eritrea's biggest challenges—and one of its biggest blights internationally.

Some native Eritreans believe that trees are supernatural and have powers that can impact humans' lives.

INTERNET LINKS

https://religionnews.com/2018/07/24/eritrea-prisoners
This article discusses the release of prisoners from shipping containers in 2018.

http://www.thearda.com/internationalData/countries/Country_76_1.asp
This pie chart displays some of Eritrea's largest religious groups.

https://www.worldatlas.com/articles/religious-faiths-and-persecution-in-eritrea.html
Learn about Eritrea's history of religious persecution.

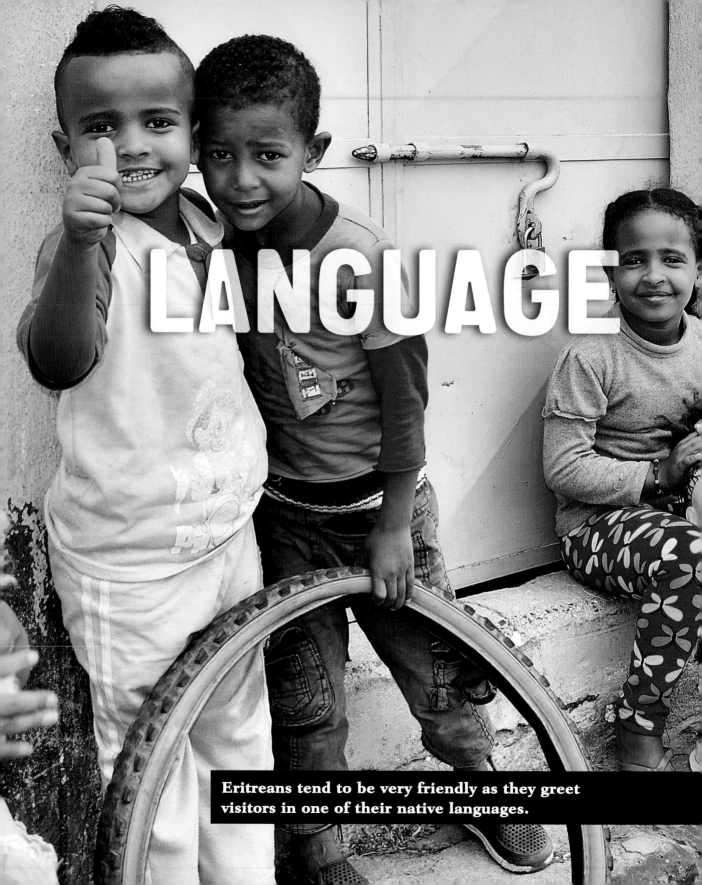

LANGUAGE

Eritreans tend to be very friendly as they greet
visitors in one of their native languages.

9

S ELAM! MARHABAAN!
Both of these words are likely
to greet visitors to Eritrea. The
first is Tigrinya, one of the three main
languages in the nation. About half of the
people in Eritrea speak this, especially
the Tigrinya ethnic group. The second
greeting is Arabic, spoken by the Muslims
of Eritrea. English is the third major
language in this country, followed by the
far less used Tigre, Kunama, and Afar.

Eritrea has no single national language, but it relies largely on Tigrinya, Arabic, and English. Eritreans are also proud of their indigenous languages. During the years of the Ethiopian occupation, Amharic, one of the main languages of Ethiopia, was made the official language, and Eritrean languages were banned. However, most Eritreans refused to speak Amharic. Instead, they continued to teach their native language to their children. Their attachment to Tigrinya became a political statement of their resistance to the occupation.

A DIFFICULT LANGUAGE

Tigrinya is a guttural language that may sound quite gruff and harsh to those hearing it for the first time. Many Tigrinya words are pronounced at the back of the throat.

Tigrinya is spoken throughout parts of Ethiopia and Sudan, as well as in Eritrea. It is based on the ancient language of Geez. As a Semitic language, it is related to Hebrew and Arabic.

ሀለሐመሠረሰቀ
በተጎነአከከወዐዝ
የደገጠጸጸፀፈ ፐ

Tigrinya is challenging to speak and to learn because it has so many grammatical rules, as well as more than 200 individual characters that represent different sounds. The consonants, such as *g* and *k*, are usually hard, and *r* is always slightly rolled on the tongue. The combination *ts* is sounded on the tip of the tongue as in the English word "pits." The vowels are pronounced either short or long. The vowel *u*, for example, is long, as in the English word "rude," while the vowel *e* is short, as in the English word "bed."

The oldest available written text in Tigrinya is the Code of Logo Sarda, a set of local laws from the 13th century. However, texts were not widely published in Tigrinya until the 19th century. A notable early publication was a Tigrinya translation of Christian Gospels in 1866. Publications such as these were aided by the sociolinguistic work of European settlers in Eritrea. The language is now spoken by around 70 percent of the Eritrean population.

A related language is Tigre, which is believed to be a direct descendant of Geez. However, Tigre and Tigrinya are not mutually intelligible. Tigre uses the same script as Tigrinya but varies in pronunciation and usage, depending on the geographical origin of the speaker.

A MUSLIM LANGUAGE

Arabic is spoken by almost half of Eritreans. It is the native language of the Rashaida tribe, and many Tigre speak Arabic in addition to their native tongue. The Muslim portion of the population needs to know the language in order to read the Quran. The use of Arabic is spreading as refugees continue to return from Sudan and the Middle East, bringing with them their mastery of the language. Like Tigrinya, Arabic is full of guttural tones and sounds made in the back of the throat. The language contains three short and three long vowels. Words always start with a single consonant followed by a vowel. The Arabic

script, consisting of 28 letters representing consonants, is written from right to left. The shape of each letter varies depending on whether the letter falls at the beginning, middle, or end of a word.

Arabic writing used in the Quran is one of the most artistic and unique scripts in the world.

GOOD MANNERS

No matter what language they use, Eritreans are friendly and are known to approach foreigners in the street to ask where they are from and how they like Eritrea.

The expected greeting at formal meetings is to shake hands with each person, asking about his or her health and family. Close friends of the same gender kiss each other on both cheeks. Former fighters, however, have the most unique greeting style: They clasp their right hands together and bump

their shoulders three times. In Arabic-speaking regions, friends who have not seen one another for a while greet by touching right cheeks, then left cheeks, and right cheeks again.

Eritreans rarely thank others for little favors. This is perhaps because the literal translation of "thank you," *yekeniely* (YUH-ke-nee-lih) in Tigrinya, sounds too solemn for everyday situations. Besides, Eritreans do not expect thanks for the small favors they do for others.

Greetings in Eritrea are commonly very friendly.

INDIGENOUS LANGUAGES

Each ethnic group in Eritrea has its own language. These minority languages belong to two main groups—the Cushitic and Nilotic—but they may share no similarities, even within their individual language group. Furthermore, each language may have several dialect variations.

Afar, Beja, Bilen, and Saho are Cushitic languages. Afar and Saho are closely related. Beja is considered one of the oldest languages in the Cushitic group. It is interesting to note that in the Beja language, the word *tigre* means "slave." For the Beja people, the Tigre language itself is associated with being a servant. Bilen, spoken mainly in and around Keren, uses the Geez script.

Believed to be among the earliest languages in Eritrea, Kunama and Nera belong to the Nilotic group. Although both use Latin script, the two languages are mutually unintelligible, and Nera speakers speak Tigre or Arabic to communicate with the Kunama. There is considerable dialect variation within Nera. Although some languages spoken in Sudan are related to Nera, Kunama has no known related language. There are some who consider Ilit, spoken in a region in the western lowlands, to be a relative, but others describe Ilit as a Kunama dialect. Barka is the main Kunama dialect and is understood by all Kunama Eritreans.

Most minority-language speakers are bilingual, especially those who have attended high school. Bilen youth, for example, mix their speech with Arabic. In general, many Christians who speak minority languages are bilingual in Tigrinya, while Muslims are bilingual in Tigre or Arabic.

LANGUAGES FROM VISITORS

One look at the city of Asmara and its architecture is enough to prove that Italy has had a huge influence on Eritrea. This is also apparent in the nation's language. Many older Asmarinos use Italian in their everyday conversations with friends of the same age. General conversation is commonly peppered with Italian words and phrases. Shop signs in Asmara and other big cities sport Italian names. However, it is in food-related industries that the use of Italian words is most pronounced, as Eritreans have adopted the Italian names for foods that do not feature in their traditional cuisine. For example, "cheese" and "carrots" are *formaggio* and *carote*, respectively—exactly as they are in Italian—but tomatoes are *pommidere*, not *pomodori*.

More and more English words have made their way into Eritrean speech today, especially in the fields of business and technology. The use of English has become more widespread in the country as more children learn the language from middle school onward and as the country has progressed and opened up to the rest of the world.

THE INFLUENCE OF MEDIA

The Eritrean government exercises strict control over the media in the country. Dissension is not tolerated, and the media are expected to portray the government in a good light. If there is criticism, journalists may face an indefinite time in jail without a trial. According to the Committee to Protect Journalists (CPJ), Eritrea is the most censored country in the world.

In 2001, the government shut down seven newspapers, effectively ending the country's private, independent press. Shortly after, the government also imprisoned more than two dozen journalists. In 2019, a number of those journalists were still behind bars. The only newspapers being published in

Eritrea serve as a mouthpiece for the government, and less than 2 percent of the population has access to the internet. Courtney Radsch, advocacy director of CPJ, says, "Eritrea is really close to an information black hole. There is virtually no independent journalism there. The government uses a combination of repressive tactics, physical and digital repression, and censorship to restrict basically any sort of independent information from getting in or out of the country. It restricts the movement of any journalist. And the only real ability to cover the country is by exiled media."

The country has a government-owned television station broadcasting on two channels and two radio stations that emit on three channels.

There are few places in the world that put as many limitations on the press as Eritrea.

Television broadcasts cover the whole country, but very few people in rural areas have access to a television set. Eritreans living in cities get to watch bulletins from international agencies such as CNN and the BBC, but only after they have been reviewed by the government. Radio reaches most of the rural population and is the best way to pass along information and promote education.

In 2009, a new radio station by and for Eritreans was launched in Paris, France, thanks to an Eritrean journalist named Biniam Simon who fled to France from his home country in 2007. His dream for an Eritrean station was helped by Reporters Without Borders. Radio Erena is an independent station that connects Eritrean exiles to their home country. It focuses on those living outside Eritrea, but also on what is happening inside the nation's borders. News is provided in both Arabic and Tigrinya. In 2017, the station was given an award by One World Media. At the time, one of the radio station's journalists, Amanual Ghirmai, said, "On this occasion, I felt Radio Erena's voice won over 'the fear,' which is the Eritrean government's preferred instrument for silencing its citizens. I am so proud of Radio Erena's team for their fight to expose the realities in Eritrea and at the same time remain independent. I hope, one day Radio Erena will be able to broadcast from Asmara." Despite the balanced news that Radio Erena provides, the Eritrean government continues to object to its broadcast, even going so far as to hack its website and jam its satellite signal.

Much of the news Eritreans hear on the radio is government-sanctioned. It is only through special stations outside the country that they can hear more accurate and updated news.

INTERNET LINKS

https://www.aljazeera.com/topics/country/eritrea.html
Catch the latest news stories and features about Eritrea from TV news source Al Jazeera.

https://cpj.org/reports/2019/09/10-most-censored-eritrea-north-korea-turkmenistan-journalist.php
Learn about the 10 most censored countries in the world, including Eritrea, from the Committee to Protect Journalists.

https://erena.org/category/eng
See what stories and news are being covered by Radio Erena at their website.

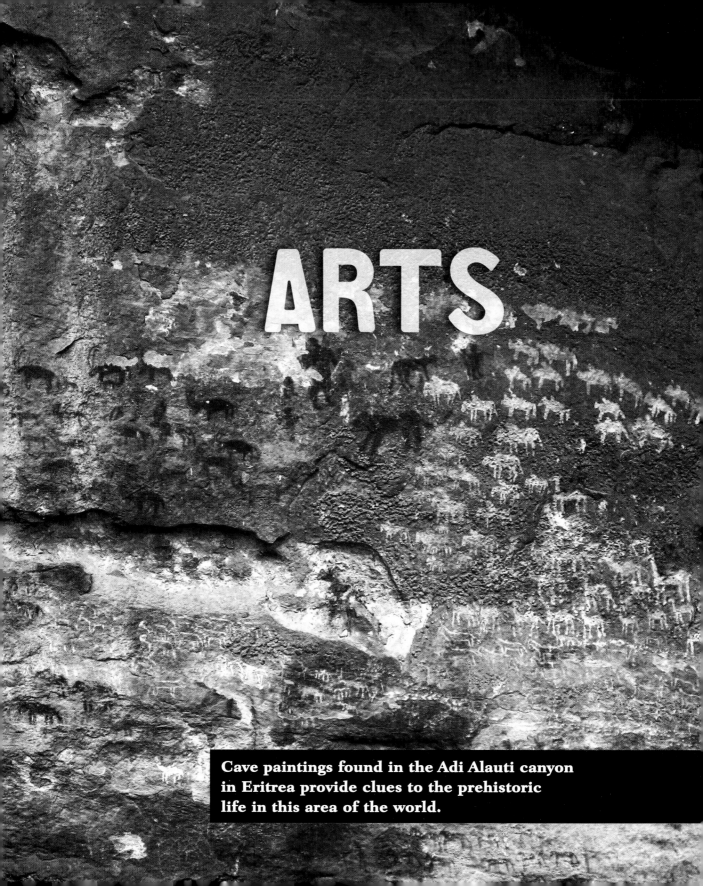

ARTS

Cave paintings found in the Adi Alauti canyon in Eritrea provide clues to the prehistoric life in this area of the world.

10

A S BARREN AND DESOLATE AS Eritrea may appear, it also is known for having one of the highest concentrations of archaeological sites in Africa. Most of the sites in Eritrea are found in the Saho region, where everything from ancient rock paintings and ruined buildings to pottery and monuments have been found. Rock paintings date back to 2000 BCE, while stone tools reach back to 8000 BCE. It seems the roots of the arts in Eritrea go back thousands of years.

Eritrea's rock art paintings feature the colors red, black, yellow, and white. Experts believe the paints were made by mixing natural elements such as charcoal, chalk, and minerals with blood, urine, egg yolks, or tree resin.

MAKING PROGRESS

Progress in the arts has been limited in Eritrea, as other issues have taken precedence. Before independence, most art was limited to nationalistic images of fighters and patriotic songs of protest. Many artists in the country still draw inspiration from their struggle for freedom and still define themselves as witnesses of the liberation war.

Nevertheless, the collection of diverse cultures in this new nation has sustained the existence of a colorful tapestry of traditional handicrafts, music, dance, paintings, and poems. The various foreign influences since the time of the Turkish invasion have also left their artistic imprint on

The impact of Italy's occupation is still clear in many of Asmara's buildings, including this one from the 1930s.

the architecture of the old buildings that still stand in the main towns. The colonial era, in particular, saw a blooming of the arts, with a distinct penchant for Italian styles. Asmara itself, with its beautiful buildings and monuments, looks like an open-air art deco museum.

As Eritrea develops economically, local artists are finding more room and opportunity to express themselves, not only to their fellow citizens but also to the world at large. An Art Lovers Club in Asmara brings together highly creative people who meet to showcase their talents and learn from one another. Art exhibitions are also staged on a regular basis in the capital as well as in Massawa.

ON THE EASELS

Most contemporary paintings before 1983 portrayed the ubiquitous EPLF flag or the body of a dead soldier. They were a very effective medium of propaganda in uplifting the spirits of the people, but they did little to advance the cause of art. Eritrean artists did not start exploring their cultural heritage and local landscapes in their creations until President Afwerki exhorted them to diversify their subject matter.

Many Eritrean artists never received formal training beyond, perhaps, a few workshops under the tutelage of the EPLF army's single professional artist during the liberation years. Consequently, their straight-from-the-heart art combined raw, primitive talent with real, spontaneous emotion. During the war, painters coped with the scarcity of art materials by blending their own paints from leaves and using sacks of wheat flour covered in milk powder as canvases.

Three of Eritrea's most recognized artists in the 20th and 21st centuries are Michael Adonai, Ermias Ekube, and Yegizaw Michael. Adonai, who trained for three years through the EPLF art program, has had art shows throughout the world and won the Raimok art award in 2002. Ermias Ekube helped to found the Asmara School of Fine Arts in 1994 and has written books on art for school students. Yegizaw Michael, known as "Yeggy," is a painter who organized Artists

Against AIDS in Eritrea in 1997. This initiative saw the joining of local artists to educate people on HIV/AIDS prevention and treatment and to destigmatize people with the condition. His murals are found on the sides of banks, homes, restaurants, museums, and theaters on two continents.

ACROSS THE PAGES

Eritrean literature has taken off slowly. Folk tales and legends have been passed down largely through oral tradition. Although the country has its store of scholarly writings, those from before the 20th century are in Geez, a dead language that only Orthodox Christian Eritreans still come into contact with when attending church services. Books sold in stores are mainly in Tigrinya and Arabic. Books in English used to be available at the British Council Library; however, it closed in 2011.

Murals, like this one found between Asmara and Keren, often portray the fight for independence from Ethiopia.

The first novel written in Tigrinya was *A Story of a Conscript* by Ghebreyesus Hailu. Written in 1927 but published in 1949, it tells the story of a group of Eritreans forced to fight for the Italians in Libya. Other novels that followed were also based on the same themes of opposition to colonialism and family relationships.

Independent Eritrea is nurturing many native authors, who write in their native tongues. Writers and poets are producing increasing amounts of poetry, fiction, and drama. One of the best known is Alemseged Tesfay, a lawyer turned historian and novelist who fought in the war against Ethiopia. Several of his plays and short stories were translated into English. A poet who writes in both Tigrinya and English is Reesom Haile. His first English-language collection was *We Have Our Voice*, which was also recorded as a CD with the poet's own voice. A number of other authors have written about their lives in a country that struggles for survival and has been so often at war. In 2005, British journalist Michela Wrong published *I Didn't Do It for You*, a book that combines her own experiences in Eritrea with the story of the nation's time under the control of Italy and Britain, and then its fight for independence.

Eritrean author Hannah Pool wrote *My Father's Daughter: A Story of Family and Belonging*, a memoir of being adopted from one of the nation's orphanages and being given the chance to connect with a long-lost brother. Another memoir penned by an Eritrean-born author is *Heart of Fire: One Girl's Extraordinary Journey from Child Soldier to Soul Singer* by Senait Mehari. As Genet Sium, an Eritrean author of multiple books, stated during an interview, "Books are being published and history is being uncovered. And this is very encouraging as we are still beginners in this area. We have a very rich language and culture that waits to be written about again and again. Thus, let us write and learn from others' experience to preserve our heritage."

Senait Mehari, mostly known by her first name alone, is a writer and singer from Eritrea.

WITH NOTES AND BEATS

The Asmara Music School had its first graduates in 1994. The school sprang from an EPLF project, which was initiated around 15 years earlier and aimed to preserve the country's musical traditions by teaching the children music. In 2019, the school's graduating class consisted of 16 students who had gone through three years of training.

For many years, all Eritrean musicians had to submit the lyrics of their songs to the government for official approval. Anything that spoke out against the government or was lacking in sufficient patriotism was often rejected by the "evaluation unit." It was frustrating and disappointing for many musical artists. That changed in 2016, however, when a new minister of information lifted this censorship rule. Today, it is much easier to release songs when no approval is needed, especially when it can be done directly on sites like YouTube. Eritrean music video producer Yonatan Tewelde says, "YouTube caters to the new Eritrean pop genre and has brought to the spotlight a line-up of young pop artists getting to the stage with seasonal hits." The Eritrean government, however, has not sat idly by as Eritreans speak out against their nation and its regime. In 2017, producers, directors, and owners of many YouTube channels were arrested. They were held for nine months without trials before being

AN AWARD WINNER

In 2018, Eritrean musician Kaleab Teweldemedhin won the Shamot Award for best song and best music video. Teweldemedhin is known for his ability to hit exceptionally high notes. Born in Asmara, he writes fondly of his homeland and his childhood. He served in the nation's military corps and, while there, was struck by a bullet in the head. During his hospitalization and recovery, he turned to music.

These experiences inspired Teweldemedhin to write about his fellow Eritreans. In a 2018 interview, he stated, "Our identity as a people is really special. Perhaps it is our history—our long years of ardent desire for sovereignty and our culture of togetherness that makes us fond of who we are no matter where life leads us. It all starts with playing together, having meals together and listening to the tales of the elders." When asked what message he had for his young fans, he added, "I want to remind them to always love our country and be proud of who they are."

released. As Abraham Zere wrote for the news platform *African Arguments*, "Given its tight control over Eritrea, President Afwerki's government may still be able to convince or coerce some musicians into singing praise songs. The question, however, is whether there is anyone left willing to listen to them."

Traditional Eritrean music uses a lot of percussion and string instruments. Drums are important in setting the rhythm for the melody provided by the *kirar* (KEE-rahr) or

Music is one way people can connect and celebrate, even in Eritrea.

the *chira wata* (CHEE-ruh WAH-tuh), the local lyre and violin, respectively. The kirar has five or six strings, each able to produce one note. Folk music is very popular in both urban and rural areas. A performance is always well attended, and members of the audience often show their enthusiasm and appreciation by climbing onto the stage to kiss and hug the performers. It is also common for Eritrean fans to dance and sing along with their musical idols, or to stick banknotes on the foreheads or in the hands of the performers.

Eritrean dancing is mainly feet-shuffling and shoulder-jerking. It looks like a cross between African and Asian dance, accompanied by mild music with loud drumming. Every ethnic group has its own dance style, and the most beautiful dancers come from the Kunama tribe. They dance in couples, freely expressing their emotions through graceful, and sometimes suggestive, moves. Tigre and Bilen women dance the *sheleel* (SHO-leel) in groups, swinging their long plaited hair vigorously across their faces.

MADE BY HAND

Every ethnic group in Eritrea has a handicraft specialty. The Nera tribe is famous for saddles and baskets. Young Nera girls learn how to make coiled baskets from their mothers. These baskets are customarily made from natural materials, but contemporary versions have incorporated yarn in vibrant colors. The baskets are used at weddings and other celebrations.

This Eritrean basket is one of many sold in stores and markets in Asmara.

Men in the Beni-Amer tribe within the Beja ethnic group always carry on them a cross-shaped dagger, which they make themselves. A curved, two-edged blade and a big, ebony hilt give the dagger a distinctive shape, which displays a strong Arabic influence.

Jewelry is another traditional handicraft. Silversmiths in the region around Keren create beautiful ornaments, which they sell in the market. Eritrean women of all ethnicities are very fond of silver and gold necklaces, bracelets, and belts.

This penchant for adornment that many ethnic groups in the country share extends to adding color wherever possible. Color is a defining characteristic of many indigenous handicrafts. Besides baskets, mats, and *injera* (bread) tray covers, even the clothes that the Eritreans wear display a myriad of colors. Rashaida dress, in particular, is multicolored and decorated with beads. Baby carriers have shells sewn onto them.

Carvings are a traditional handicraft shared by all the ethnic groups in the country. Using basic tools and raw materials such as wood and clay, sculptors create an assortment of figures, including human and animal shapes, bowls, and trays.

Colorful jewelry is often added to outfits for special occasions in Eritrea.

ON THE STAGE

Drama is an ancient art form in Eritrea and was traditionally staged to celebrate religious festivals. During the war for independence, the EPLF performed short skits all over Eritrea to stir up local resistance against Ethiopian oppression. Today, theater is growing more popular in Eritrea as a channel of artistic expression.

In Asmara, foreign classics are staged regularly in native languages at the Opera House. A production of Henrik Ibsen's *A Doll's House* running from 2009 to 2010 was performed in Tigrinya by actors from the PFDJ Cultural Group in cooperation with the Norwegian government. To bring the play closer

The performing arts are growing in other ways today—for example, at festivals. The annual Eritrea Festival, held in Asmara, has a different theme each year. In 2019, it was Resilience for Higher Progress. Zemede Tekle, the commissioner of culture and sports in Eritrea, stated that the festival would showcase both the culture and traditions of smaller ethnic groups throughout the nation as well as provide musical performances, children's programs, and an art show.

to the Eritrean audience, the characters' names were changed to local ones, and the play was carefully adapted to a contemporary Eritrean middle-class context. Conversely, Alemseged Tesfay's *The Other War* has been performed in the English language in Europe and appeared in an English anthology of African plays.

A number of the productions performed in Eritrea are done to show the effort it took to gain freedom for the nation and its people.

Eritrea is making progress in creating its own works for the stage. With a traditional foundation in dance and music, indigenous theatrical groups supported by international cultural organizations are gradually integrating native dance and music with modern dramatic skills. The various ethnic groups are also exploring their cultural heritage to write plays in their own languages.

Prior to the closing of its Eritrean branch in 2011, the British Council was one foreign organization that actively contributed to the development of theater in Eritrea. In 1997, it collaborated with two other foreign bodies to run two training courses for native artists.

In 2019, a movie called *Luce* was released. Starring Naomi Watts, Tim Roth, Octavia Spencer, and Kelvin Harrison Jr., it is a thriller about an Eritrean child soldier who is adopted by an upper-middle-class couple from the United States.

INTERNET LINKS

https://www.goodreads.com/topic/show/634368-eritrea
See a list and discussion points about a selection of books written by Eritrean authors and books set in Eritrea here.

https://www.latimes.com/local/lanow/la-me-nipsey-hussle-south -eritrea-south-los-angeles-20190407-story.html
Read about the life and death of Nipsey Hussle, a singer with direct ties to Eritrea.

https://www.theguardian.com/world/2015/aug/19/eritrea-music- history-eplf-youtube-viral-pop
This article explores more about the history of Eritrean music in the past and present.

https://www.youtube.com/results?search_ query=Kaleab+Teweldemedhin+
Listen to some of Kaleab Teweldemedhin's music on his YouTube page.

LEISURE

Coffee plays a huge role in Eritrea as a way of honoring guests.

N A COUNTRY WHERE THE WEATHER IS unreliable, food is often scarce, liberty is threatened, and work rarely stops, there is little opportunity for relaxation or leisure. However, Eritreans make the most of what they have. Children still play in between chores, often doing hand games and singing songs. Pretending is another way to play and learn, as boys and girls imitate loading camels or harvesting crops. In the larger cities, young people often spend time in cafés, go to see a movie, shop, or drop in at a recreational center.

CAPITAL CITY SIGHTS

Those living in the capital city are typically much luckier than those living in the rural areas when it comes to socializing. In addition to going to the movies and hanging out at cafés, they can go to plays, concerts, and dances.

The National Museum is a place that attracts locals as well as tourists. It has multiple sections, including an archaeological area, an art gallery, a natural history section, and a medieval history section. The ethnography section features handicrafts by the nation's different ethnic groups, while the archives section has documentation about all of the items in the different collections.

AT THE MOVIES

Going to the movies used to be considered a decadent activity in Eritrea, associated with a life of luxury. Since independence, however, the government has stressed the importance of film as a constructive art form with educational and recreational value. Ticket prices have been kept low to make movies affordable to more Eritreans. Movie theaters in Asmara have been renovated to offer more comfortable seating and better projection equipment. The smaller towns, however, still make do with open-air cinemas. Owning a home movie-watching system does not seem to keep Eritreans away from the movie theaters, where they can catch the latest Hollywood blockbusters and Arabic dramas. However, tight censorship cuts out scenes that are considered politically subversive or physically revealing.

The Asmara Indie Film Festival began in 2018, started by Sephora Woldu and Elilta Tewelde, who are Eritrean American filmmakers, and it continues today. The festival takes place in September in the United States, but its ultimate goal is to be held in Asmara itself. The theme of the festival centers around finding one's place in the greater world.

The National Museum is a wonderful place for locals and visitors to learn about Eritrean history.

EXPERIENCES FOR THE YOUNG

Government-run youth clubs are important meeting places for young people in cities. They organize educational as well as recreational programs, such as woodwork or metalwork for young men and sewing or home economics for young women. Debates, quizzes, and other competitions test the members' general knowledge.

The National Union of Eritrean Youth and Students (NUEYS) is a nongovernmental organization whose mission is to build a "versatile youth." It is mainly an educational group, with members taking part in environmental conservation initiatives and health education. It conducts seminars and campaigns on youth empowerment and raises awareness of gender issues, particularly girls' education. Members also take part in recreational and sporting activities.

The Cinema Impero in Asmara is one of the most beautiful movie theaters in the country.

THE COFFEE CEREMONY

In Eritrea, having a cup of coffee, or *bun* (BOON), is not something done on the run and without much thought like it is in other countries. Instead, it is an elaborate, traditional social activity. The preparation is always the woman's job. She often begins by burning incense. Once everyone is seated, she sits down on a low stool and roasts the raw coffee beans in a shallow, metal pan over a small charcoal fire. The smoking beans are passed around to the guests so they can smell the aroma. The hostess and the guests use their hands to waft the smoke toward their faces.

When the house is filled with the wonderful smell of roasted coffee beans, the hostess grinds the beans in a mortar using a pestle. She then transfers the ground coffee into a round clay pot with a long neck and a tube-like spout. Some people add a little crushed ginger as well. The hostess pours water into the pot and brings the coffee slowly to a boil. Letting it boil over invites shame,

so as soon as the mixture starts to boil, the hostess removes it from the fire, lets it cool slightly, and then returns the pot to the fire. She repeats this step several times to attain the desired strength.

After an hour, the coffee is finally served in tiny cups with lots of sugar. Popcorn is passed around to accompany the coffee. The entire coffee-making process is repeated as many times as it takes to ensure that all the guests have had their fill. Everyone is expected to drink at least three cups and compliment the taste. A lack of praise often results in the hostess pouring away the prepared coffee and brewing a fresh pot.

ON TWO WHEELS

Cycling is not only one of the most popular sports in Eritrea—Eritrean cyclists are some of the best riders in the world. Cycling races are held almost every weekend of the year throughout Eritrea, and people are so excited to watch,

TIME FOR A RHYME

Hand-clapping games are fun for many Eritrean children. Here is one of the most common. It tells the story of a man whose love disappears. By the time he finds her, he has to go and fight in the war, so he must say goodbye again:

In Tigrinya:
Semira Semira gual Asmara
Gezana a'tseyato nabey keyda
Tekhedku-tekhedku si'inaya,
Ab ghem-ghem bahri rekibeya!
Chaw chaw chaw hadigeki
Chaw chaw chaw hadigeki
Chaw chaw chaw hadigeki
Chaw chaw chaw hadigeki
Be'al edl iyu zwesdeki!

In English:
Semira, Semira from Asmara
She closed the gate to our house, where did she go?
When I went to look for her, I couldn't find her
Later, I met her at a forest near a lake.
Bye, bye, bye, I'm leaving you
Bye, bye, bye, I'm leaving you
Bye, bye, bye, I'm leaving you
Someone luckier than me will have you.

they do not even mind inconveniences that might arise. Thousands of spectators turn out in the streets to cheer for the racers. In 2019, the city hosted the Africa Cup, a brand-new cycling competition. Damr Gebretinsae, one of Eritrea's national cycling federation's officials, says, "No weekends pass without streets being blocked for a cycling event. People are surprised if the streets aren't blocked. Cycling has become a cultural space where people meet to talk. It has become a part of city life."

ZERSENAY TADESE

One of the other sports Eritreans are becoming more well known for is long-distance running. One of Eritrea's lead runners is Zersenay Tadese. Born in 1982, Tadese held the men's world half marathon record from 2010 to 2018. On May 6, 2017, he was one of three acclaimed runners to take part in the Nike Breaking2 challenge. For two years prior, Tadese and fellow runners Lelisa Desisa and Eliud Kipchoge trained in elite training centers with one goal in mind: being the first people to run a marathon (26.2 miles; 42.2 km) in under 2 hours. Tadese and his team ran loops around an Italian track, under optimal conditions. In the end, Tadese finished second with a time of 2 hours, 6 minutes, and 51 seconds.

In addition to riding bicycles in races, many Eritreans use them simply for transportation.

Eritreans first became interested in cycling in the 1930s when they saw Italian cyclists. Within 10 years, Eritreans were beating Italians in all races. By 2015, two Eritrean cyclists were included in the Tour de France. When they came back home, they were treated as national heroes. Douglas Ryder, manager of an Africa-based cycling team, says, "Eritrea is producing the best riders at the moment and the most consistent performers across the African continent. The sport is growing phenomenally there. Eritrea is the strongest cycling nation on the African continent, they've got absolute talent and they're getting better." One of the toughest races in Eritrea takes places on the Asmara-Keren road. The 50-mile (80 km) route winds up and down steep slopes, testing and sharpening cyclists' skills.

SOCCER

When it comes to soccer, Eritreans have two reputations: one for being great players and one for defecting, or refusing to return home to Eritrea, after playing matches abroad. Members of the national soccer team, the Red Sea

Camels, defected after international games in 2007, 2009, and 2012. After the third time, the government disbanded the team, but then it came up with a new idea. They would create a new team, but this time it would be mostly made up of Eritreans already living abroad. The plan did not work, and in 2015, 10 members of the team refused to return to Eritrea. Finally, in 2019, Eritrea's government came up with another new plan. All soccer players playing in international competitions were expected to pay a huge bond and surrender their property before leaving the country. Whether or not that will be enough to convince traveling athletes to return is questionable. However, soccer players aren't alone. In the past, Eritrean cyclists, cross-country runners, and swimmers have also defected.

INTERNET LINKS

https://www.nike.com/us/en_us/c/running/breaking2/breaking2 -runners
Find out all about the Nike Breaking2 challenge, and read more about the runners involved.

http://www.shabait.com/about-eritrea/art-a-sport/6100-the -national-museum-of-eritrea
Read about the history of Eritrea's National Museum.

https://sprudge.com/video-coffee-ceremony-eritrea-51613.html
Watch *Mom's Coffee*, a six-minute film about Eritrea's coffee ceremony (with English subtitles).

https://www.youtube.com/watch?v=Q1KaxtQJ2k4
Watch a video of Eritrean cyclists winning the Tropicale Amissa Bongo race in 2019.

https://www.youtube.com/watch?v=6oygbo3TUaQ
Watch Eritrean children sing and dance to new Eritrean music.

FESTIVALS

In Asmara, people celebrate the 25th anniversary of the country's independence.

D ESPITE THE CHALLENGES Eritreans face, they still take time to celebrate. Religious and traditional festivals and holidays occur throughout the year. Even the arrival of the rains and the end of the harvest are reasons to rejoice. Most celebrations center around food, drink, music, and dancing. What is served and how people behave is largely dependent upon the type of religion behind each holiday.

HOLIDAYS FOR CHRISTIANS

On festival days, Orthodox Christians in Eritrea go to church in their best clothes. After the service, the priests lead the congregation in a street procession, and the rest of the day is spent feasting and having fun. The priests are always served the best food and wine at these feasts.

Timket is the most important festival for Orthodox Christians in Eritrea. It commemorates the baptism of Jesus in the Jordan River. The night before the holiday, people flock outdoors in lively and colorful processions. The next day, priests parade a small cloth-covered chest, symbolizing the Ark of the Covenant, through the streets. The congregation

To celebrate Timket, the priests carry golden crosses and wear elaborate robes.

follows them to a pool or river to witness the reenactment of Jesus's baptism. They celebrate with a feast after the parade.

The festival of Meskel commemorates the finding of Jesus's cross by Empress Helena (the mother of Constantine the Great) in the fourth century CE. Followers plant a tree in the town square and later bring tall branches or poles with yellow daisies tied at the top to this location. After the church service, the priests lead the congregation to the bundle of branches in the square and set fire to it. Then, everyone dances around the bonfire in celebration and sings songs.

The Kunama call the holiday of the cross Mashkela. Kunama villagers carry lit torches in procession to a clearing outside the village. Here, they pile their torches in a huge bonfire and dance around it until the last ember flickers out. Then, they gather the new harvest and prepare a drink from the fresh grain

ANNUAL CELEBRATIONS

The Eritrean government has declared 17 public holidays per year. This number may seem large, but it is the only way to ensure that the various religious groups in the country are well represented.

The National Holidays		Religious Holidays	
January 1	New Year's Day	January 7	Orthodox Christmas
February 10	Fenkil Day	January 19	Timket (Epiphany)
March 8	International Women's Day	Spring (varies)	Good Friday
		Spring (varies)	Easter Sunday
May 1	Labor Day	September 27	Meskel (Finding of the True Cross)
May 24	Liberation Day		
June 20	Martyrs' Day	December 25	Christmas
September 1	National Day	Varies	Eid al-Fitr
December 8	Children's Day	Varies	Eid al-Adha
		Varies	Mawlid al-Nabi (Prophet Muhammad's Birthday)

The dates for Good Friday and Easter Sunday vary from year to year because they are determined in relation to the cycles of the moon. However, they are always celebrated in March or April. Muslim holidays follow the Islamic calendar, whose 12 lunar months add up to years of only 354 or 355 days. Thus, holidays like Eid al-Fitr (the end of the fasting month), Eid al-Adha (the feast of the sacrifice), and Mawlid al-Nabi (the birthday of the Prophet Muhammad) do not fall on the same day of the Gregorian (Western) calendar each year, or even in the same season.

to offer their ancestors. Only after all these rituals have been performed do they eat food from their harvest.

Catholic and Protestant Eritreans pay the most attention to Christmas. On December 25, they attend services at church and then go home to feast and exchange presents among family and friends. Those who can afford it put up a Christmas tree and perhaps a Nativity scene.

MUSLIM CELEBRATIONS

The Eid al-Fitr celebration is a special one for the nation's Muslims and often involves large gatherings.

The three most important celebrations for Muslim Eritreans are Eid al-Fitr, Eid al-Adha, and Mawlid al-Nabi. Festivities for the first two can last up to 10 days in certain regions.

Eid al-Fitr celebrates the end of Ramadan, the Muslim fasting month. For 30 days, all Muslims, except for the very young, the very old, and the infirm, eat or drink nothing from sunrise to sunset. This is a time given to prayer, meditation, and introspection. On the morning of Eid al-Fitr, everyone puts on new clothes, children ask their elders for forgiveness, and the men go to the mosque for special prayers. When they come back, it is time to feast with relatives and friends. Some villages organize communal games and activities. The Beni-Amer take part in camel races and competitions showcasing their swordsmanship and horsemanship.

Eid al-Adha is one of the holiest days of the year and is a time of sacrifice. It commemorates when the ancient figure Ibrahim nearly sacrificed his son to Allah (God). Animal sacrifices characterize this festival. Muslims slaughter sheep and offer the skins at the mosques. This is also the time when people make pilgrimages to Mecca, Saudi Arabia, the holiest site in Islam. All families make it a point to visit their relatives on Eid al-Adha.

Mawlid al-Nabi commemorates the birth of the Prophet Muhammad. Although it is celebrated with as much fervor as Eid al-Fitr and Eid al-Adha, this is usually a solemn occasion. After morning prayers, all male believers gather together to enjoy cooked meat and dates with tea and coffee. The women stay at home to share a modest banquet. During Mawlid al-Nabi, Muslims recite a text describing the birth of the Prophet. They accompany their chanting with a dance.

Since Muslim holidays rely largely on the sighting of the new moon, each country may celebrate on a different day. Traditional greetings on these days are "Eid Mubarak" or "Eid Saeed."

CELEBRATING NATIONHOOD

Eritreans devote three days each year to celebrating their nationhood. National Day falls on September 1, the day the armed struggle against the

Ethiopian military regime was launched in 1961. Liberation Day, on May 24, commemorates the joyous occasion when the EPLF troops evicted the Ethiopian army from Asmara in 1993. Martyrs' Day, on June 20, remembers those who lost their lives in the fight for their country's freedom.

The program for these events contains speeches by the president and other leaders, public demonstrations, cultural shows, sports contests, seminars, and exhibitions. At the start of official celebrations, religious leaders representing the major faiths say a prayer for the country and give their blessings to the people. Public displays aim to reinforce Eritrean patriotism and to emphasize the need to be committed to rebuilding the country. As they celebrate their hard-won freedom, Eritreans are also reminded of the difficulties that lie ahead and of the contributions that each of them has to make.

Here, Eritreans celebrate the country's 25th anniversary with singing and dancing.

HONORING CHILDREN

Most festivals for children in Eritrea are religious in nature. Hiyo falls on the day after Christmas and commemorates the killing of infants by King Herod as told in the Bible. On Hiyo, children visit villagers' homes and sing for a treat of roasted chickpeas. For Aba Abraham on August 27, children parade through the streets with lighted torches. When they go home, their elders walk over the torches placed on the floor and pray for a bountiful harvest. Hoye, celebrated with burning torches, singing, and processions, takes place twice a year, on New Year's Eve and Meskel's Eve.

The festival of Aba Samuel spans two weeks in December. During this time, girls go singing from house to house, receiving food and money in return. They use part of the money to buy food, which they offer to the church. They spend the rest of the money on food for themselves, and usually everyone else joins in the feast.

At almost every wedding in Eritrea, certain foods and beverages are expected—and they have to be made well. Even a perfect wedding and reception will be insulted and scorned if the refreshments are not professionally made. One drink that is found at virtually every wedding is suwa *(SOO-wah), a beer-like beverage. Suwa takes patience and time to make, as it has to ferment for almost two weeks. It is made of grain, barley flour, and buckthorn, or gesho, leaves. These are bitter leaves that are much like the hops used in Western beer-making. The leaves must stand in water for six days. Then, the other ingredients are added, and the mixture stands for another week. When it is done, this Eritrean beverage is ready to serve to eager wedding guests.*

FOCUS ON THE FAMILY

For babies born in a Christian family in Eritrea, the first life event that is celebrated is baptism and name-giving. Baby boys are baptized at the age of 40 days, while baby girls are baptized when they are 80 days old. Early in the morning, the mother dresses herself and her baby in their best clothes and goes to church with the baby's godparents and some relatives. The baby is baptized and named following the church service, and then everyone shares some bread. At home, the parents throw a lunch party, inviting friends, neighbors, and the priest who performed the baptism. Guests typically bring sugar and bread for the baby.

In Muslim households, circumcision is the most important childhood event, done to boys around the age of seven. Circumcision is an important and a big event. Goats are slaughtered, relatives and friends come over with gifts, and much feasting takes place. In the evening, religious leaders arrive to do the operation, and the family offers them food, sweet syrup, and coffee.

Although now banned in Eritrea, girls were circumcised for many generations. This practice is a grave violation that many human rights and medical organizations, including the World Health Organization (WHO), are trying to outlaw across all societies. Today, it is being done away with across Eritrea, although slowly. As of 2010, 83 percent of Eritreans practiced female circumcision, a decrease compared to 89 percent in 2002.

Weddings usually take place in January, outside the harvest seasons and fasting periods. In the villages, betrothals and arranged marriages are still the norm, and families sometimes look for their children's life partners within their own clan. The bride's family pays a dowry, and the groom's family pays a bride price of cattle, jewels, and dresses. Weddings are considered very important events. As one Eritrean phrased it, "Once in your life you're born, once in your life you die, and once in your life you get married, so you must do it right, so as to remember it properly." Christian marriage ceremonies tend to last two days.

Weddings are reasons for families to celebrate the start of a new branch.

INTERNET LINKS

http://elearn.fiu.edu/e-dev/WorldExplorer/Customs/Africa2/eritrea.htm
Learn more about the marriage and social traditions of Eritrea from Florida International University.

https://www.weddingwire.com/wedding-ideas/african-wedding-guest
Read about some of the most common wedding customs in different parts of Africa here.

https://www.youtube.com/watch?v=-Ax5M91tV2s
Watch a traditional Eritrean wedding held in 2018.

FOOD

Eritreans like to make rich meals
with bread, meat, and spices.

WHAT IS ON THE DINNER TABLE IN Eritrea depends largely on what part of the country it is in. In the Italian-influenced city of Asmara, it is common to see platters full of pizza and pasta. Along the coast, seafood dishes, including shrimp and lobster, are typical. In the majority of smaller households, however, the most common dishes are thick stews, spongy bread, and spicy meats and vegetables.

Unfortunately, Eritrea often struggles to produce enough food to feed all of its people. Due to chronic drought, families living in rural areas stare famine in the face each day of their lives, wondering when they will see their next meal and where it will come from. Throughout the country, over 39 percent of children under the age of 5 are underweight. The majority of Eritreans depend on food aid from the international community, surviving on porridge made from ground grain, flour, and water. When they have nothing to eat, the poor fill their stomachs with anything barely edible, such as wild vegetables and prickly pears. People in the urban areas, in contrast, have access to a variety of foodstuffs.

The most commonly eaten bread in Eritrea is called injera. *This pancake-like bread is made from a grain called teff. This is found growing in Eritrea's highlands. The bread has a slightly sour taste, and its sponginess makes it both a filling food and a helpful utensil. Many Eritreans tear off pieces to soak up juices and then roll the bread up to scoop up larger chunks of meat or vegetables. The bread also helps buffer the spiciness of many of the dishes served in this nation. Another type of bread is* kitcha *(KIT-cher). It is made from wheat or barley and is baked.*

Injera is a common bread in Eritrea and other African countries.

BEYOND INJERA

The popular bread injera is often served alongside a chicken or beef stew, known as *zigni* (ZIHG-nee). Other stews typically found in Eritrea are those made with vegetables, called *alicha* (ah-LEE-cher), or with a puree made from legumes, called *shiro* (SHEE-roe).

As a general rule, people in the highlands consume teff, wheat, and barley, while those in the lowlands cook with sorghum and millet. More oil and butter is used in the urban areas because those living in the rural areas cannot afford these items.

Meat consumption is limited to the very wealthy in Eritrea. The poor get to taste meat stews only on festival days, when the village holds a feast. The most common meat is goat, but the coastal populations also consume a fair amount of fish. Rural Eritreans get most of their protein from milk and legumes such as lentils. The poor living in the urban areas of the country substitute meat

Eritrean meals often look like this: an assortment of food atop injera.

with tripe, which is made from the organs of animals such as cows, sheep, or goats. Another alternative to meat dishes is shiro. Because this porridge-like stew keeps for days, many working mothers cook a big pot during the weekend and then reheat portions of the shiro for daily meals.

Spices play an important role in Eritrean cuisine. In fact, all traditional recipes in the country require at least one type of spice, and most dishes are flavored with a combination of several. *Berbere* (bear-BEAR), a blend of numerous spices and dried chilies, goes into almost everything, from shiro to zigni.

HAVE A DRINK

Eritreans consume water, milk, and a variety of traditional drinks. Muslims generally do not drink alcoholic beverages, sticking to coffee, tea, and other unfermented drinks. Highland Muslims have a preference for *abake* (ah-BAH-kay), an unfermented drink made from a lentil-like grain. Linseed is also ground and mixed with water to make a refreshing drink.

Mead in Eritrea is a nonalcoholic honey drink. Its fermented version is *mies* (MEES). Because of the high cost of honey, it is not as popular as the other homebrew, *suwa* (SOO-wah), a beer-like drink made from a combination of grains and special leaves that resemble hops. *Zebib* (ZAY-bib) is an anise-flavored liquor that Eritreans usually bring with them when visiting their friends or relatives. The Afar make a very strong alcohol, called *douma* (DOE-mah), from the sap of palm trees.

Carbonated drinks are also enjoyed by young and old in Asmara and in other towns. Besides the ubiquitous Coca-Cola and other soft drinks, Eritrean urbanites like to drink *spritzi* (SPRIT-zee), which is fizzy water flavored with fruit juice. Adults enjoy tea or espresso, always with a lot of sugar. In some areas, coffee is served with ginger or black pepper as well as with sugar. Blended banana, mango, or papaya juices are also common in the major cities.

MANNERS AT THE TABLE

Eritrean families eat communal-style, sharing food from a large tray placed in the middle of a low dining table. Children and adults sit at separate tables, especially among the Tigrinya, as the former are considered to have no table manners. Before a meal, one of the women of the household goes around carrying a basin of water, in which everyone washes their hands. This is because Eritreans eat with their fingers.

Everyone gathers around a low table, sitting on stools or the floor, and then the head of the family says a prayer. Each person takes from the portion of food closest to him or her, using only the right hand. It is considered bad manners to lick the fingers or let fingers touch the lips. Leftover food on the plate should never be returned to the communal tray. When everyone is done eating, a prayer of gratitude is said once again. Finally, the wife removes the food from the table, as the rest of the family continues to praise the food and murmur thankfulness for their blessings.

IN THE KITCHEN

Cooking is done by women only, especially in the rural areas. The kitchen is a small and dark space located in a small hut away from the living quarters. Few houses have running water, and one of the most important utensils is the water pot. Girls walk for hours every day to fetch water from the communal well or tap. The stove is placed on the floor, and the cook either squats or sits on a low stool to prepare meals. Most rural kitchens are equipped with wood-burning stoves, while in the towns, people use charcoal for fuel. Only the very rich families can afford gas or electricity.

Urban cooks use aluminum pots and pans, while many rural women still use utensils made of clay or wood. However, plastic spoons and bowls are becoming more common in rural kitchens. The mortar and pestle—a large ceramic or stone bowl and a long pole—have disappeared completely in the towns but can still be found in rural kitchens. Women spend a long time each day grinding the grains for making injera or porridge.

TO THE MARKET

Fresh produce can be obtained from the many markets in Eritrea's rural and urban areas. Large villages and small towns in the country hold weekly

Cactus fruit, also known as prickly pear, is frequently sold at local markets in Eritrea.

markets that attract people from places as far as 5 miles (8 km) away. These people come to sell their excess subsistence crops and home-reared livestock, and to pick up food supplies. Eritrean markets have everything. Although stalls selling meat, fruits, vegetables, grains, and spices are the focus of activity, market-goers can also find furniture, kitchen utensils, clothes, jewelry, and religious artifacts being sold at stalls standing on the outskirts of the main market. Surrounding the market in Keren, for example, are tailor shops and vendors of various handicrafts.

Asmarinos have the added option of patronizing supermarkets and grocery stores. The wealthier residents can even buy fine wines and chocolates from specialty Italian-style shops.

GOING OUT TO EAT

Eritreans eat out mainly at lunchtime, when it is impractical to prepare their meals. Dinner, however, is usually eaten at home, as it is much cheaper to eat in. Only wealthy families can afford to dine out regularly. In the evenings, the restaurants in Asmara and Massawa are mostly filled with tourists, foreign residents, and diplomats.

Most restaurants in Eritrea serve either local or Italian food. The fare may not always be up to international standards, owing to the lack of trained cooks and high-quality ingredients. Far more popular than the restaurants in Asmara are the cafés that dot the city. Some of these open early in the morning to sell breakfast favorites, such as scrambled eggs with onions and tomatoes, called *frittata* (FRI-ta-tah), and *fool* (FOOL), a bean puree. Asmarinos love to sit at the sidewalk cafés, where they chat with their friends over carefully prepared coffee, watching the people and traffic go by. Many cafés are equipped with a television, and this draws in large evening crowds for ice cream or after-dinner drinks.

Repeated droughts throughout Eritrea have made it incredibly difficult for its people to grow what they need to eat to live and thrive. The problem is only increased by the government's continued denial of international aid and, in fact, denial that any food shortages ever existed in the first place. This unwillingness to admit that the country needs help will only continue to make life in this small African nation that much harder.

INTERNET LINKS

http://www.asmera.nl/asmara-markets.htm
This website explores different markets around Asmara.

http://www.eritrea.be/old/eritrea-cuisine.htm
This website describes popular Eritrean ingredients and foods, and provides photos of some of the delicious meals.

https://www.theguardian.com/food/2018/oct/06/yotam -ottolenghi-eritrean-ethiopian-recipes-berbere-vegetables -teff-flatbread
This column from the *Guardian* explores different popular Eritrean and Ethiopian dishes.

WAT (LENTIL STEW)

Lentils are often eaten in Eritrea, although only the most wealthy families add any type of meat to the dish.

Makes 8 servings
½ cup oil
1 onion, chopped
5 cloves garlic, chopped
2 carrots, chopped
1 15-ounce can chopped tomatoes
1½ cups lentils (red or green)
2 cups water or stock
Salt and pepper to taste

Heat oil in a pan, and sauté onion and garlic until brown.

Stir in the carrots, tomatoes, and lentils.

Add water (or stock), salt, and pepper, and stir thoroughly together.

Bring to a boil, then simmer on low heat, covered, until the lentils are tender (approximately 40—45 minutes).

Serve with a side of buttered toast or crackers.

HABESHA GOMEN (SAUTÉED GREENS)

Greens like kale, chard, or spinach have many vitamins and minerals and help provide nutrition when food is limited.

Makes 4 servings
1½ tablespoons oil
4 cloves garlic, minced
½ onion, diced
1 bunch greens (kale, chard, spinach)
1½ tablespoon soy sauce
Pepper to taste
2 tablespoons water

In a frying pan, heat the oil over medium heat.

Add the onion and garlic, and sauté for 2 minutes, stirring often.

Add in the greens, and sauté another 2 to 3 minutes.

Add in the soy sauce, pepper, and water.

Reduce heat, stirring the greens until they are tender (about 5 minutes).

Serve hot with stew and/or bread.

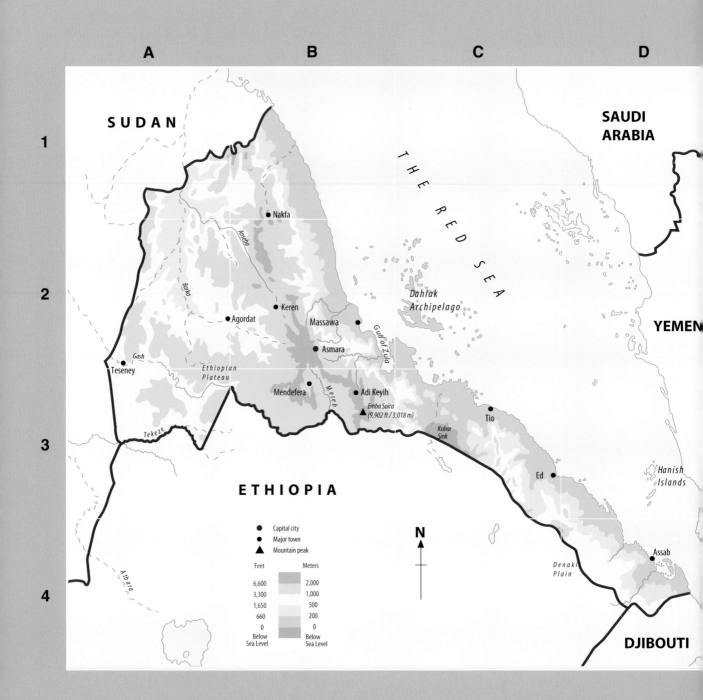

A   B   C   D

SUDAN

SAUDI ARABIA

1

THE RED SEA

2

• Nakfa

Anseba

Barka

• Keren

Agordat •

Massawa •

Dahlak Archipelago

Asmara •

Gulf of Zula

Gash

Teseney •

Ethiopian Plateau

Mendefera •

Mereb

Adi Keyih •

Emba Soira
(9,902 ft / 3,018 m)

Tio •

Kobar Sink

YEMEN

3

Tekeze

Ed •

Hanish Islands

ETHIOPIA

• Capital city

• Major town

▲ Mountain peak

N

Denaki Plain

Assab •

Atbara

Feet   Meters

6,600   2,000

3,300   1,000

1,650   500

660   200

0   0

Below Sea Level   Below Sea Level

4

DJIBOUTI

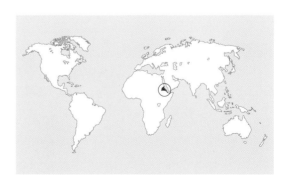

ECONOMIC ERITREA

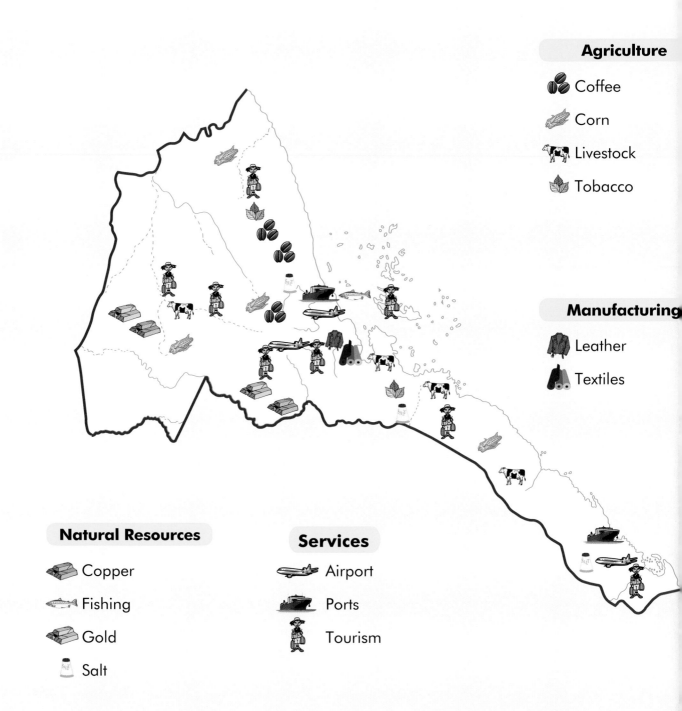

Agriculture

- Coffee
- Corn
- Livestock
- Tobacco

Manufacturing

- Leather
- Textiles

Natural Resources

- Copper
- Fishing
- Gold
- Salt

Services

- Airport
- Ports
- Tourism

ABOUT THE ECONOMY

All figures are 2017 estimates unless otherwise noted.

OVERVIEW

The Eritrean economy has suffered greatly from wars and many years of drought. Today, it is trying to rebuild but accomplishing that goal slowly. The economy relies mostly on mining for its economic output, although agriculture employs 80 percent of its population. Still, unreliable rainfall makes crop output difficult to gauge from year to year, and not enough food is produced to feed the Eritrean populace. In 2013, the government updated its banknotes in hopes of stemming currency issues overseas. Although a member of the UN Human Rights Council, Eritrea remains one of the most oppressed nations in the world, and its reputation has made tourists hesitant to visit.

GROSS DOMESTIC PRODUCT (GDP)
$9.402 billion

GDP PER CAPITA
$1,600

GDP GROWTH RATE
5 percent

CURRENCY
Nakfa (ERN)

ERN TO USD
$1=15 ERN (2019 estimate)

INFLATION
9 percent

LABOR FORCE
2.71 million

NATURAL RESOURCES
gold, potash, zinc, copper, salt, oil and natural gas, fish

AGRICULTURAL PRODUCTS
sorghum, lentils, vegetables, corn, cotton, tobacco, sisal, livestock, goats, fish

INDUSTRIES
food processing, beverages, clothing and textiles, light manufacturing, salt, cement

TOURISM
107,000 visitors (2011 estimate)

MAIN EXPORTS
gold and other minerals, livestock, sorghum, textiles, food, manufactured goods

MAIN IMPORTS
machinery, petroleum products, food, manufactured goods

MAIN TRADE PARTNERS
China, Italy, Turkey, Saudi Arabia, South Africa, South Korea, United Arab Emirates

CULTURAL ERITREA

Nakfa Trenches
Shoulder-deep trenches stretch over 25 miles (40 km), meandering across the hillside of Denden. Here, a whole town was built underground as the center of the resistance to Ethiopian rule in the 1980s. Five to six fighters lived in underground bunkers not larger than 3.3 by 6.5 feet (1 by 2 m), sleeping, eating, and fighting for 18 months at a time. An incredible memorial to human endurance and courage, Nakfa and Denden's trenches are remembered by all Eritreans.

Semenawi Bahri National Park
Located at an altitude of between 2,300 and 6,560 feet (700 and 2,000 meters), Semenawi Bahri (also called Filfil National Park) is the last remnant of Eritrea's tropical rain forest. Here, vervet monkeys and hamadryas baboons are easily seen, as well as gazelles, bushbucks, warthogs, and even leopards. A wide variety of birds make their home in the forest too.

Debre Bizen
The Orthodox Monastery of Debre Bizen was founded in 1368. Its library contains more than 1,000 manuscripts as well as various church relics, including crowns, robes, and incense burners. Situated at 8,040 feet (2,450 m) above sea level, the monastery is not open to women or any female creature.

Water Cisterns
One of Eritrea's most ancient relics, the water cisterns number 365, one for every day of the year. Cut from the coral limestone, they catch rainwater and provide the main source of fresh water for the Dahlak Islanders. More than 1,000 years old, some are still in use.

Enda Mariam Orthodox Cathedral
This cathedral displays a blend of Italian and Eritrean architecture. The massive horizontal stone beams are examples of traditional Aksumite architecture as well as traditional stones used as bells. Lovely murals depicting scenes from the Bible adorn the inside walls.

The Stele
Dating from the middle of the first century BCE, the Stele is a structure measuring 15.35 feet (4.68 m) above ground and 3.3 feet (1 m) below. It is unique in Eritrea with its pre-Christian symbol of the sun over a crescent moon. A Geez inscription down the middle dedicates the stele to King Agheze's forefathers. The area around Metera is an important archaeological site that predates the Aksumite period in some parts. Excavations have unearthed gold objects dating to the second century CE as well as Mediterranean amphorae and marble plates.

Lake Badda
Lying below sea level, beautiful Lake Badda was formed in the crater of an extinct volcano, Abuhibet. This turquoise jewel at the edge of the Danakil Depression measures 1,312 feet (400 m) in diameter and, according to an old Italian survey, is 328 feet (100 m) deep. The opposite wall of the crater is solid lava.

ABOUT THE CULTURE

All figures are 2018 estimates unless otherwise noted.

OFFICIAL NAME
State of Eritrea (*Hagere Ertra*)

CAPITAL
Asmara

TOTAL AREA
45,406 square miles (117,600 sq km)

POPULATION
5,970,646

ADMINISTRATIVE ZONES
Anseba, Central, Gash-Barka, Northern Red Sea, Southern, and Southern Red Sea

MAJOR CITIES
Asmara, Keren, Massawa, Assab, Mendefera, Barentu

MAJOR RIVERS
Anseba, Barka, Gash, and Tekeze

MAJOR LANGUAGES
Afar, Arabic, Tigre, Kunama, Tigrinya, English, and other Cushitic languages

ETHNIC GROUPS
Tigrinya 55 percent, Tigre 30 percent, Saho 4 percent, Kunama 2 percent, Rashaida 2 percent, Bilen 2 percent, others 5 percent (2010 estimate)

MAJOR RELIGIONS
Sunni Muslim, Orthodox Christian, Roman Catholic, Protestant

BIRTH RATE
29.1 births per 1,000 people

DEATH RATE
7.1 deaths per 1,000 people

INFANT MORTALITY RATE
Total: 44.4 deaths per 1,000 live births
Male: 51.4 deaths per 1,000 live births
Female: 37.3 deaths per 1,000 live births

FERTILITY RATE
3.9 children born per woman

LIFE EXPECTANCY
Total population: 65.6 years
Male: 63 years
Female: 68.2 years

TIMELINE

IN ERITREA	IN THE WORLD
125,000 BCE Early humans settle near Bay of Zula south of Massawa.	
1000 BCE Tribes from present-day Yemen migrate to the southern highlands of Eritrea.	**753 BCE** The ancient city of Rome is founded.
600 BCE Arabs visit the coast of Eritrea.	
300–600 CE Eritrea is part of the Ethiopian kingdom of Aksum.	
400 Christianity arrives with Syrian merchants.	
600–700 Arabs introduce Islam to coastal areas.	**1206–1368** Genghis Khan unifies the Mongols and starts
1500s Ottoman Empire annexes Eritrea.	conquest of the world. At its height, the Mongol Empire under Kublai Khan stretches from China
1577 The Sultanate of Awsa, an Afar sultanate, is founded in southeast Eritrea.	to Persia and parts of Europe and Russia. **1776**
1869 Italian priest Giuseppe Sapeto buys Assab from local sultan.	The US Declaration of Independence is signed.
1890 King Umberto of Italy declares colony of Eritrea, with Massawa as the capital.	**1914** World War I begins.
1935 Mussolini invades Abyssinia from Eritrea, using chemical weapons.	**1939** World War II begins.
1941 British forces defeat Italians at Keren and take over administration of Eritrea.	**1945** The United States drops atomic bombs on Hiroshima
1946 Italy formally renounces all claims to its African colonies.	and Nagasaki, Japan. World War II ends.
1948 Four Powers Commission fails to agree on Eritrea's future.	

IN ERITREA	IN THE WORLD
1952 Eritrea is federated with Ethiopia under UN-brokered deal.	
1961 Armed struggle begins.	
1962 The Eritrean parliament is dissolved. Ethiopia formally annexes Eritrea.	**1963** Civil rights leader Martin Luther King Jr. delivers his "I Have a Dream" speech in Washington, DC.
1991 EPLF takes Asmara.	
1993 Formal independence is reached. Isaias Afwerki becomes president of Eritrea.	
1997 Eritrea launches its own currency, the nakfa.	**1997** Hong Kong is returned to China.
1998 Border war with Ethiopia begins.	
2000 OAU peace treaty is signed. UN peacekeepers patrol temporary security zone between Eritrea and Ethiopia.	**2001** Terrorists crash planes in New York; Washington, DC; and Pennsylvania.
2003 Boundary commission rules that the disputed border town of Badme lies in Eritrea. Ethiopia rejects the ruling.	**2003** War in Iraq begins.
	2005 Hurricane Katrina destroys major parts of New Orleans.
	2008 Barack Obama wins the United States presidency.
	2016 Donald Trump wins the United States presidency.
2017 UNESCO names Asmara to its list of World Heritage sites.	
2018 Eritrea and Ethiopia officially reconcile.	
2019 President Afwerki forces all athletes to pay a bond and sign over property deeds before allowing them to leave the country to compete internationally.	**2019** Hurricane Dorian destroys huge parts of the Bahamas.

GLOSSARY

abake (ah-BAH-kay)
An unfermented drink made from a lentil-like grain.

amba (AHM-bah)
A small tableland with steep walls and a flat top.

amulet
A charm usually worn from a necklace that some think possesses magical abilities.

animism
A religion in which its followers consider everything within the natural world, including animals, plants, and rocks, to have a soul.

chira wata (CHEE-ruh WAH-tuh)
A musical instrument similar to a violin.

defect
To refuse to return to one's home country, often for political reasons.

diaspora
The movement or scattering of a group of people from their established homeland.

douma (DOE-mah)
A very strong alcohol made by the Afar from the sap of palm trees.

exorcise
To carry out a religious practice where a devil or evil spirit is said to be removed from a person's body.

kirar (KEE-rahr)
A harp-like instrument with five or six strings.

kitcha (KIT-cher)
A very thin unleavened bread baked from wheat or barley.

mies (MEES)
An alcoholic beverage made with honey and water.

quno (KOO-noh)
A hairstyle in which the hair is plaited, or braided, in fine strands close to the scalp and left loose from the nape.

sheleel (SHO-leel)
A group dance in which women shake their long plaited hair vigorously across their faces.

yekeniely (YUH-ke-nee-lih)
A Tigrinya expression of gratitude; literally means "may God keep you."

zigni (ZIHG-nee)
A chicken or beef stew.

FOR FURTHER INFORMATION

BOOKS

Bereketeab, Redie. *The Ethiopia-Eritrea Rapprochement: Peace and Stability in the Horn of Africa*. Uppsala, Sweden: The Nordic Africa Institute, 2019.

Giorgis, Andebrhan Welde. *Eritrea at a Crossroads: A Narrative of Triumph, Betrayal and Hope*. Houston, TX: Strategic Book Publishing and Rights Agency, 2014.

Plaut, Martin. *Understanding Eritrea: Inside Africa's Most Repressive State*. Oxford, UK: Oxford University Press, 2017.

WEBSITES

Britannica. "Eritrea." https://www.britannica.com/place/Eritrea.

CIA. *The World Factbook*. "Eritrea." https://www.cia.gov/library/publications/the-world-factbook/geos/er.html.

Eritrea.be. http://www.eritrea.be/old/eritrea-information.htm.

FILMS

Hager Alatni. Directed by Yonas Mihretab, 2017.

Heart of Fire. Directed by Luigi Falomi, 2008.

Life is Fare. Directed by Sephora Woldu, 2018.

Mallets in the Mountains—The Eritrean Railway. Produced by Highball Productions, 2010.

Tigisti. Directed by Daniel Tesfamariam, 2012.

BIBLIOGRAPHY

Ahmed, Hadra. "Ethiopian-Eritrea Border Opens for First Time in 20 Years." *New York Times*, September 11, 2018. https://www.nytimes.com/2018/09/11/world/africa/ethiopia-eritrea-border-opens.html.

Araia, Tesfalem. "Remembering Eritrea-Ethiopia Border War: Africa's Unfinished Conflict." BBC News, May 6, 2018. https://www.bbc.com/news/world-africa-44004212.

Bekit, Teklemarian. "Eritrea's Catholic Church 'Dumbfounded' by School Seizures." BBC News, September 11, 2019. https://www.bbc.com/news/topics/cz4pr2gdgjyt/eritrea.

Cawthorne, Andrew. "Eritrea's Mangroves Show Way to Fight Hunger." Reuters, May 22, 2008. https://uk.reuters.com/article/feature-etritrea/eritreas-mangroves-show-way-to-fight-hunger-idUKNOA23276420080522.

CIA. *The World Factbook*. "Eritrea." https://www.cia.gov/library/publications/the-world-factbook/geos/er.html.

Dumais, Eliza. "Model Grace Mahary is Powering Eritrean Homes with Solar Energy in Between Runway Shows." *Yahoo Lifestyle*, July 9, 2019. https://www.yahoo.com/lifestyle/model-grace-mahary-powering-eritrean-150500539.html.

"Eritrea Keeps Mandatory National Service Despite 'Peace'—HRW Worried." *Africa News*, March 13, 2019. https://www.africanews.com/2019/03/13/eritrea-keeps-mandatory-national-service-despite-peace-hrw-worried.

"Eritrea Mine Action." Landmine and Cluster Munition Monitor, November 10, 2017. http://www.the-monitor.org/en-gb/reports/2017/eritrea/mine-action.aspx.

Pruitt, Sarah. "Archaeologists Discover Possible Homo Erectus Footprints in East Africa." History.com, September 6, 2018. https://www.history.com/news/archaeologists-discover-possible-homo-erectus-footprints-in-east-africa.

"The Status of the Constitution of Eritrea and the Transitional Government." ERI-Platform, October 23, 2018. https://eri-platform.org/updates/status-constitution-eritrea-transitional-government.

Steff, Brittany. "Eritrean Gazelles: Once Lost, and Now Found in Their Namesake Country." Global Wildlife Conservation, July 19, 2019. https://www.globalwildlife.org/blog/eritrean-gazelles-once-lost-and-now-found-in-their-namesake-country.

United National Development Programme. "A Shining New Example for Eritrea." UNDP.org. http://www.er.undp.org/content/eritrea/en/home/ourwork/environmentandenergy/successstories/greening-undp-eritrea.

Voice of America, "Rights Groups Urge Release of Journalists in Eritrea." Big News Network, September 19, 2019. https://www.bignewsnetwork.com/news/262462449/rights-groups-urge-release-of-journalists-in-eritrea.

INDEX

INDEX